The Heinemann Science Scheme

Book 3

Ian Bradley • Peter Gale • Mark Winterbottom

Heinemann

This book is dedicated to the following people:

From Ian Bradley: To Deb, Sam and Julia for their tolerance, and Pip for being quiet between meals.

From Peter Gale: To Mum and Dad, for the freedom to explore.

From Mark Winterbottom: To Sal, for being brilliant.

Heinemann is an imprint of Pearson Education Limited, a company incorporated in England and Wales, having its registered office at Edinburgh Gate, Harlow, Essex, CM20 2JE.
Registered company number: 872828
Heinemann is a registered trademark of Pearson Education Ltd

First published 2002

ISBN 978 0 435582 53 1

13
13

Edited by Mary Korndorffer

Designed and typeset by Cambridge Publishing Management Ltd

Illustrated by Hardlines

Printed and bound by CPI Group (UK) Ltd, Croydon, CR0 4YY

Index by Paul Nash

Acknowledgements
The authors and publishers would like to thank the following for permission to use photographs:
Cover photo of Skydiver on snowboard, Getty Images/Stone; Firecracker (linked chain of bangers), SPL/Erich Schrempp; Oak tree, false colour, SPL/Dr. Jeremy Burgess.

p2 T: Tempsport/Corbis, M (L-R): Ecoscene, Ed Young/Corbis, Ted Spiegal/Corbis; **p4** L and R: SPL; **p6** T (L-R): Papilio/Mikael Svensson, B: Ecoscene; **p7** T (L-R): Richard Hamilton-Smith/Corbis, Ecoscene, Archivo Incongrafico/Corbis, M: Ecoscene/Derrick Beavis, B: Photodisc; **p8** L and R: Peter Morris; **p9** T and B: SPL; **p10** T: Ecoscene, B: Ed Young/Corbis; **p11** T (L-R): Peter Morris, B: SPL; **p12** T: Photodisc, B: Joseph Sohn/Corbis; **p13** Corbis; **p14** Duomo/Corbis; **p16** T and M:

Peter Morris, B: Lawrence Maning/Corbis; **p17** Photodisc; **p19** SPL; **p20** R and L: SPL; **p21** Gareth Boden; **p23** Ecoscene/Andrew Brown; **p24** Gareth Boden; **p25** T: Garden matters, Photodisc, Photodisc, SPL, Peter Morris; **p26** T and B: Gareth Boden; **p29** L and R: Ecoscene; **p30** Ecoscene/Anthony Harrison; **p31** T-B: Peter Morris, Gareth Boden, SPL, Michael Boys/Corbis; **p32** T: Peter Morris, B (L-R): Ecoscene, Environmental Images; **p34** L and R: SPL; **p35** Ed Young/Corbis; **p36** L-R: Ecoscene/Robin Redfern, Papilio/Ken Wilson, Ecoscene/Chinch Gryniewicz, Ecoscene/Robin Williams, Papilio/Robert Pickett; **p38** Ecoscene/Michael Howes; **p39** Environmental Images/Toby Adamson; **p40** Gareth Boden; **p41** T-B: Gareth Boden, Felix Zaska/Corbis, Roger Ressmeyer/Corbis, Beken of Cowes, Ecoscene; **p42** Gareth Boden; **p43** L: Frank Lane/Corbis, R: Peter Morris; **p44** Gareth Boden; **p45** Peter Morris; **p46** Gareth Boden; **p47** T: Gareth Boden, B: Peter Morris; **p48** Gareth Boden; **p49** T: Peter Morris, B: Kit Houghton/Corbis; **p52** T: Kevin Morris/Corbis, Avaldo De Lucia/Corbis, Corbis, M and B (L-R): Gareth Boden, **p54, 55, 57, 58** and **59** Gareth Boden; **p60** T: Arne Hodalic/Corbis, M: James Amos/Corbis, B (L-R): Corbis, Paul Soulders/Corbis; **p61** Kevin Morris/Corbis, M (L-R): Gianni Dagli Orti/Corbis, Gareth Boden, B: James Amos/Corbis, **p62** (T-B) Ecoscene/Corbis, Michael Brusselle/Corbis, Ecoscene, Holt Studios, Ecoscene, Ecoscene; **p63** T and B: Ecoscene, **p64** (T-B) Ecoscene, Environmental Images, Corbis/Michael Nicholson, Corbis/Roger Wood, Ecoscene; **p64** Environmental Images; **p66** and **67** Gareth Boden; b T and M (L and R): Gareth Boden, B (L and R): Ecoscene; **p70** T: Corbis, B: Gunter Marx/Corbis; **p72** Michael Yamashita/Corbis; **p73** T (L-R) Stephanie Maze/Corbis, Ginny Stroud-Lewis, Peter Morris, Shout Pictures, B: Peter Morris; **p74** T (L-R): Ecoscene, Jeffrey Rotmann/Corbis, Peter Morris, Paul Souders/Corbis, B (L-R): Peter Morris, Peter Morris, Environmental Images; **p75** SPL; **p76** T (L-R): Peter Morris, Corbis, M (L-R): Corbis, Corbis, B (L-R): Corbis, Peter Morris; **p77** L: Ecoscene, R: Environmental Images; **p78** Gareth Boden; **p79** T and M: Gareth Boden; B Gareth Boden; **p82** T: Peter Morris, B: Peter Gould; **p85** Environmental Images; **p95** Gareth Boden ; **p96** Gareth Boden; **p98** T and B: Corbis, **p99** Photodisc; **p101** Photodisc; **p103** Gareth Boden; **p104** T: Ales Feuzer/Corbis, B: Gareth Boden; **p105** Mike King/Corbis; **p106** T: Kevin Morris/ Corbis, M-B: Gareth Boden; **p107** T-B: Gareth Boden. Gareth Boden, Peter Morris; **p108** L-R: PaulSoulders/Corbis, Ecoscene, Ecoscene; **p109** Ecoscene; **p110** T: Photodisc, B: Kevin Morris/ Corbis; **p112** Robert Holmes/Corbis; **p114** Gareth Boden; **p115** Corbis; **p116** Gareth Boden; **p117** and b Peter Morris; **p119** Keely Mooney/Corbis; **p120** Ecoscene; **p121** T: Photodisc, B: Robert Harding.

(T = Top, M = Middle, B = Bottom, L = Left, R = Right)
SPL = Science Photo Library

Picture research by Ginny Stroud-Lewis

The publishers have made every effort to trace the copyright holders, but if they have inadvertently overlooked any, they will be pleased to make the necessary arrangements at the first opportunity.

Welcome to Heinemann Science Scheme!

This is the third book in a series of three which covers all the science you need to learn at Key Stage 3.

It is divided into twelve units. Each unit has topics which take up a double page spread. On each double page spread you will find:

● **A topic checklist at the start with this heading:**

> **TOPIC CHECKLIST**

This tells you what you will study on that double page spread.

● **Questions as you go along like this:**

> **ⓑ What is the solute in salt solution?**

These are quick questions which help you check that you understand the explanations before you carry on.

● **Questions in a box at the end of the spread with this heading:**

> **QUESTIONS**

These help you draw together all the material on the spread.

Important words are highlighted in bold on the pages. They all appear in a glossary at the back of the book with their meanings so that you can look them up easily as you work through the book.

As you study Heinemann Science Scheme you will also be doing practical activities and extra questions and assignments from the teacher's pack which goes with it, as well as tests which help you and your teachers keep track of how you're doing.

We hope you enjoy studying science with Heinemann Science Scheme.

Contents

A Inheritance and selection

WHAT CAUSES VARIATION: INHERITANCE

TOPIC CHECKLIST

- What characteristics can be inherited?
- How are characteristics inherited?
- Why are children of the same parents not identical to each other?

What characteristics can be inherited?

Look at the picture of the Brazilian football team. They all have different characteristics. Their characteristics vary.

All animals and plants **inherit** some characteristics from their parents. Look at the pictures below.

(a) Write down two characteristics that the calf has inherited from its mother.

(b) Write down one characteristic that the baby plants have inherited from their mother.

How are characteristics inherited?

It is possible to inherit characteristics from *both* your mother *and* your father. This is because a new human being is made when a **sperm cell** from the father meets an **egg cell** from the mother. The two nuclei join in **fertilisation**.

(c) Did the girl inherit her dark hair from the mother or the father?

(d) Did the boy inherit his thin eyebrows from the mother or the father?

Family tree

The nucleus of the sperm and the egg carry information from the parents. The information is carried by **genes**. When the nuclei join together, the genes from the sperm and egg join together. Because genes control certain characteristics, you may inherit a gene for blue eyes, or for blonde hair. Because you get genes from each of your parents, you can inherit characteristics from each of your parents. This is called **inherited variation**.

Why are children of the same parents not identical to each other?

Look at the family tree again. Because the boy and girl have both inherited genes from the same set of parents, you would expect them to look quite similar. But they do not look exactly the same. Each child has inherited different genes from its mother, and different genes from its father, to create a new combination of genes. Each child is a unique person, not exactly like its brothers and sisters, but not completely different either.

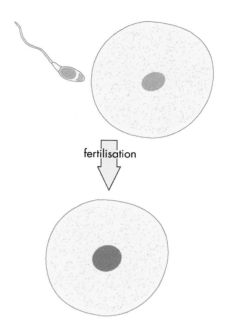

fertilisation

The nucleus of the sperm cell and egg cell carry genes

QUESTIONS

1 What does inherited mean?

2 Why are brothers and sisters more similar to each other than to children of other parents?

3 For fertilisation to happen, an egg and a sperm need to meet. The zygote produced then develops into an embryo. How are the egg and sperm adapted to their functions?

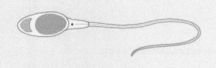

Sperm cell

Egg cell

WHAT CAUSES VARIATION: ENVIRONMENT

Why do identical twins look the same?

Unlike all other children, identical twins are born looking exactly the same. They look the same because they have the same genes. Look at what usually happens to a zygote after fertilisation has happened.

When identical twins are formed, the sperm and egg join together as usual, but as soon as the zygote starts to divide, it splits apart into two completely separate cells. Each one starts to develop independently to form a new baby. Because each cell has the same genes, the children produced are identical.

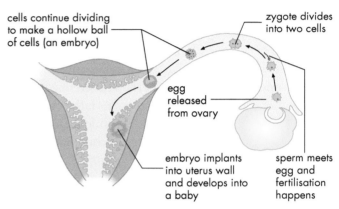

cells continue dividing to make a hollow ball of cells (an embryo)

zygote divides into two cells

egg released from ovary

embryo implants into uterus wall and develops into a baby

sperm meets egg and fertilisation happens

Fertilisation for one child

a Can identical twins be different sexes?

What is environmental variation?

Although identical twins may look the same when they are born, they soon begin to look different. Look at the pictures of the twins as babies and then as adults.

The adult twins look different because their characteristics have changed during their lives.

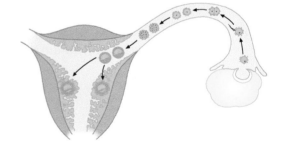

Formation of identical twins

- One twin has cut her hair whereas the other has grown her hair long.
- One twin has a very active job, which helps her to stay very thin, whereas the other works in an office, and does not take as much exercise.

This type of variation is called **environmental variation**. It can be caused by a living thing's surroundings, by what it eats, what it drinks and how it lives.

b What is the difference between environmental and inherited variation?

These identical twin babies look very similar...

...but identical twin adults can look different

How do inherited variation and environmental variation affect living things?

Most characteristics of the human body are affected by both inherited variation and environmental variation. Environmental variation does not change your genes; it simply changes your characteristics.

Imagine a person who has genes to make them tall, fat and intelligent.

Their environment can still affect these features.

- They will not be tall if they do not eat a balanced diet.
- They will not be fat if they do not eat enough food.
- They will not be intelligent unless they go to school.

Inherited and environmental variation can also combine to affect characteristics in plants. Class 9Z6 at King Edward School decided to investigate variation in two different varieties of tomatoes. For each variety, they measured the mass of 20 tomatoes and plotted them on a graph.

They saw an obvious difference between the masses of the two varieties. Such a big difference is almost certainly caused by genes.

- The beefsteak tomatoes have inherited genes that make them large.
- The cherry tomatoes have inherited genes that make them small.

But look at how the mass of the tomatoes in each variety also varies. Such variation is likely to be caused by the environment. Tomatoes of both varieties have grown in different environmental conditions.

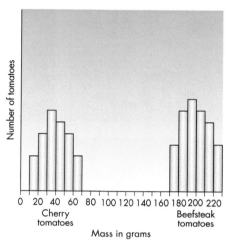

Histogram of tomato mass for beefsteak and cherry tomatoes

QUESTIONS

1 a How many times does fertilisation happen when identical twins are made?

b Explain why identical twins are born identical.

c Why do identical twins begin to look slightly different as they get older?

2 Make a list of environmental factors that may cause variation in **a** humans and **b** plants.

SELECTIVE BREEDING IN ANIMALS

TOPIC CHECKLIST

- How are new breeds of animal produced?
- Why do farmers produce new breeds of animal?
- Why are some breeds conserved?

How are new breeds of animal produced?

Look at the photographs of the different breeds of dog. They are said to be different breeds because they look very different.

ⓐ Write down one characteristic for each breed, which you could use to recognise it. For example, the Dalmatian would be recognisable by its spots.

Breeders like to exhibit their dogs at dog shows. By choosing which mother and father will produce offspring, breeders can affect the appearance of the dogs that they take to the show. This is called **selective breeding**.

Exhibiting at a dog show

For example, if a breeder wanted a Dalmatian with lots of spots, she would choose two parents with lots of spots, and make them breed together. Because the puppies would inherit genes from both parents for 'lots of spots', they would also be likely to have lots of spots. By choosing or selecting parents with a particular inherited feature, and breeding them together, the dog-breeder has produced the offspring that she wants.

ⓑ Jack has a male and female dog, both of whose hair he has cut short. Jack has heard of selective breeding and thinks that the offspring of these two dogs will also have short hair. Explain why he is mistaken.

Selective breeding is used not only for producing attractive-looking dogs. Humans have used selective breeding for centuries. Look at the dogs in the pictures below.

The huskies have been bred for their strength and stamina to pull sleds. The sheepdogs have been bred for their intelligence and ability to herd sheep. The greyhounds have been bred for their speed for hunting.

Why do farmers produce new breeds of animal?

Modern farm animals have been created by selective breeding over hundreds of years.

- Dairy cows (e.g. Friesian) have been bred to produce lots of milk.
- Sheep have been bred to produce lots of wool.
- Pigs have been bred to produce lots of meat.

Sometimes, farmers actually mix two different breeds to get the desirable characteristics they want. Hereford bulls produce high quality meat. Hereford bulls are often bred with Friesian cows to improve the meat quality of the Friesians' offspring. The offspring are easily identifiable by their white face, which they also inherit from the Hereford bull.

Hereford bull

Why are some breeds conserved?

Humans have bred animals for thousands of years. During that time needs have changed. For example, tastes in meat have changed, and customers now prefer to buy lean meat rather than fatty meat. Because of changes like this, many breeds are no longer farmed commercially. However, they may still have useful genes, which we might want to use in the future. Such genes may make them resistant to harsh weather conditions or disease. To make sure these genes do not die out, and are available for breeding in the future, rare-breed centres have been set up around the country to conserve these animals.

Friesian cow

QUESTIONS

1 What is selective breeding?

2 Why have dogs been selectively bred?

3 Explain what you would do to breed sheep for wool quality.

4 Write a newspaper article about why rare-breed centres have been set up around the country.

SELECTIVE BREEDING IN PLANTS

Why do plant breeders do selective breeding?

In your local supermarket there are lots of different varieties of fruit and vegetables. Many of these varieties have been produced by selective breeding.

Many fruit and vegetables have been bred to look nice or to taste nice. But there are other qualities that are important to farmers and customers.

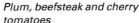

Plum, beefsteak and cherry tomatoes

Iceberg, cos and curly lettuces

- If a vegetable plant is resistant to cold weather, it can be planted earlier in the year and be ready for sale earlier. A farmer will make more money by selling more vegetables during the year.

- If vegetables are resistant to rotting, they can be transported further from the farm before they rot. This means the farmer will make more money by sending his vegetables to more and more shops further away, even abroad.

How does fertilisation happen in plants?

Fertilisation happens inside flowers. Female egg cells are found inside ovules in the ovary. Male **pollen cells** are found inside pollen grains, which are made by the anthers. Pollen grains are either carried by insects or blown by the wind from an anther of one flower to the stigma of another flower.

Pollination happens when a pollen grain arrives at the stigma. A pollen tube grows from the pollen grain, down the style and into the ovary, where it joins up with an ovule. You can see a pollen tube growing, in the photo on the next page. After this, fertilisation happens: the pollen cell travels down the pollen tube so the pollen cell nucleus joins up with the egg cell nucleus in the ovule. This makes the first cell of a new plant. This new cell divides and divides to form an embryo and a seed. This seed can grow into a new plant.

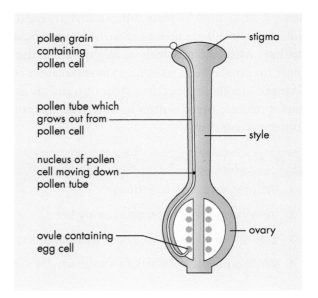

How do plant breeders do selective breeding?

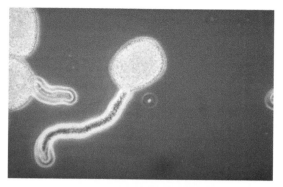

Plant breeders do selective breeding just like animal breeders. They choose the parents with the desired characteristics and breed them together. However, because plants will not mate together on their own, plant breeders must transfer the pollen grains between flowers themselves.

That sounds easy, but there can be some problems with plant breeding on a large scale:

- Pollen from other flowers may reach the stigma of the parent plant. To stop this happening, breeders often put the parent plant inside a plastic bag before and after transferring the pollen.

- Anthers and stigma may mature at different times. A pollen tube can only grow down into a mature stigma. Because of this, plant breeders sometimes have to store pollen, and transfer it to the stigma when it has become mature.

- It is impossible to see the results of plant breeding immediately. The breeder must harvest the seed and grow it to see if they have been successful. This can be very time-consuming.

By brushing pollen from the anthers of one flower to the stigma of another, the pollen is successfully transferred.

QUESTIONS

1 Write down three characteristics that may be chosen by plant breeders.

2 What is the difference between pollination and fertilisation?

3 Write a set of instructions for a trainee plant breeder. These should include how to carry out the procedure, and what, if any, precautions they need to take.

WHAT IS A CLONE?

TOPIC CHECKLIST

- What is asexual reproduction?
- How are clones produced?
- Why are people worried about cloning?

What is asexual reproduction?

Most plants reproduce using pollen cells and egg cells (**sexual reproduction**). Some plants do not do this. Instead, they use **asexual reproduction**. This means they simply grow a new baby plant, which eventually separates itself from its parent. Look at the spider plant. It has grown a baby which is ready to separate from its parent.

Because they have been made directly from only one parent, they have the same genes as that parent: they are genetically identical. We say they are **clones** of their parent.

Spider plant

How are clones produced?

When plant breeders produce a perfect plant with all the characteristics they want, it would be useful to have a clone of that plant. Many plants make clones of themselves when they reproduce asexually. Look at the strawberry plants. They produce long stems, which grow sideways from the parent. Wherever these stems touch the ground, a new set of roots and leaves emerges, and makes a new strawberry plant, which is a clone of its parent.

ⓐ **If a parent and its clone look different, what is the cause: inherited or environmental variation?**

Strawberry plants

Gardeners and breeders can also produce clones themselves by taking cuttings. Because they cut the twig directly from the parent, it is genetically identical to the parent, and forms a clone of the parent. Look at the photographs to find out how a breeder does this.

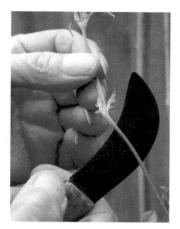

She cuts a twig from the parent plant

She dips the end in rooting powder

She plants the twig in a new pot. Soon the new plant grows roots and leaves, exactly the same as the parent plant

ⓑ Explain why a cutting is a clone of its parent.

Animals can also be cloned, but this is more complicated than with plants. The picture shows Dolly the sheep, who was cloned from her mother at a research institute in Scotland.

Why are people worried about cloning?

Although cloning seems to have many benefits, it does cause some concern amongst scientists and the general public.

Dolly the sheep

- All the individuals made by cloning are identical. This means they are all susceptible to the same diseases. If a particular disease killed off one plant in a farmer's crop, it would kill all the plants. This would be very bad news for a farmer.

- Many people believe that cloning is not natural, or that it goes against their religion. Some people are worried that a scientist may one day try to clone a human being. Because of this, politicians have made human cloning illegal in many countries around the world.

QUESTIONS

1 Why are clones genetically identical to their parent?

2 Why do plant breeders often use cloning to produce new plants?

3 Write a script for a TV reporter, explaining the good things and the bad things about cloning.

B Fit and healthy

WHAT DO WE MEAN BY FIT?

TOPIC CHECKLIST

- What is fitness?
- How do we release energy from food?
- Why is diet important?

This person looks very fit

What is fitness?

Fitness is actually a measure of how well your heart and lungs deliver oxygen to the cells around your body. To get fit, many people embark on a **fitness programme**, telling them how much exercise to do, what to eat, and how to cut down on alcohol and cigarettes. Fitness programmes are designed differently for different people, because their bodies respond differently.

You can measure fitness in several different ways. You might:

1   Find out your heart rate when you are at rest.

2   Find out how long it takes your heart rate to return to normal after 30 seconds of exercise.

3   Press a set of bathroom scales with your arms raised up and measure how hard you can push.

Some people say they are fit if they successfully take part in a marathon

 **a   What is fitness?**

How do we release energy from food?

All of your cells need oxygen, so they can release energy from glucose by **respiration**. Look at the word equation:

$$glucose + oxygen \xrightarrow[\text{energy is released}]{} carbon\ dioxide + water$$

To supply glucose and oxygen to the cells around your body, the **digestive system**, **breathing system** and **circulatory system** need to be working properly.

- Glucose is in the food you eat. It is absorbed into the blood in the digestive system.
- Oxygen is in the air you breathe. It is absorbed into the blood in the lungs (the breathing system).
- Both glucose and oxygen are carried around the body in the blood through the circulatory system. The heart pumps blood around the body.

Why is diet important?

You do not need only glucose in your food. You need a **balanced diet**, containing all the nutrients your body needs to stay healthy.

Nutrient	Function in body
Carbohydrates (e.g. glucose)	Energy
Fats	Energy, warmth
Protein	Growth and repair, energy
Vitamins	Keep you healthy
Minerals	Keep you healthy
Fibre	Keeps your digestive system working properly
Water	Chemical reactions in your body need water to happen

It is important that you eat the correct amount of each nutrient. For example, if you eat too much fat, you may become obese and very unfit. Fats collect inside your blood vessels, narrowing the space inside for blood to flow. This puts a strain on the heart, because it has to work harder to pump blood around your body.

However, if you eat too little fat and carbohydrate, you can also become very ill. Look at the boy in the picture to find out why.

An unbalanced diet may have other effects on children. Their growth and development are often slow, and also they are more likely to get ill. An unbalanced diet means that you are not eating enough of some particular nutrients. This is called a **deficiency**. Look at the list to find out the problems this can cause.

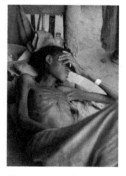

Because he does not eat enough fat and carbohydrate, he has used up all the protein in his muscles for energy.

Nutrient deficiency	What happens if you do not eat enough?
Protein	Kwashiorkor: liver and pancreas stop working properly.
Folic acid	Spina bifida: a baby's spinal cord does not develop properly in its mother's womb.
Vitamin C	Scurvy: gums and skin go soft and start to bleed.
Calcium	Rickets: teeth and bones become soft.
Zinc	Growth and development may be slowed down.
Iron	Anaemia: blood does not carry oxygen properly, and you become pale and tired.

QUESTIONS

1 What is the name for 'the release of energy from food'?

2 Explain why you need protein, fat and carbohydrate in your diet.

3 What is meant by a balanced diet?

4 Write an advertisement for folic acid tablets. Your advert should include information for pregnant mothers to explain why they should take the tablets.

THE BREATHING SYSTEM AND SMOKING

TOPIC CHECKLIST

- How do we breathe?
- What controls our breathing?
- How does cigarette smoke affect your body?

How do we breathe?

When your body's cells respire, they need oxygen, and they need to get rid of carbon dioxide. We breathe to take oxygen into the blood and remove carbon dioxide from the blood. Breathing is controlled by intercostal muscles between the ribs, and by the diaphragm muscle under the ribs.

When we breathe in, the rib cage lifts and moves outwards. The diaphragm muscle moves downwards. This increases the space inside the chest, making more space for air to rush in.

When we breathe out, the rib cage lowers and moves inwards. The diaphragm muscle moves upwards. This reduces the space inside the chest and pushes air out of the lungs.

What controls our breathing?

You can control how quickly and deeply you breathe.

Look at the sprinter. Because she is exercising, her muscle cells need energy and she needs to respire more quickly. Because of this, she breathes more quickly and deeply to get the extra oxygen required.

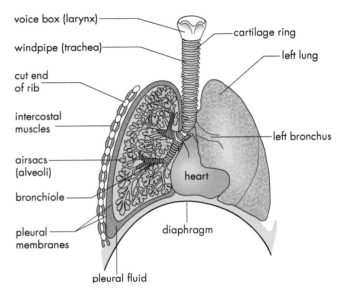

Cross-section of thorax

(voice box (larynx), windpipe (trachea), cut end of rib, intercostal muscles, airsacs (alveoli), bronchiole, pleural membranes, pleural fluid, cartilage ring, left lung, left bronchus, heart, diaphragm)

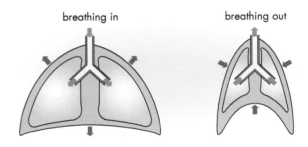

breathing in   breathing out

ⓐ Explain why you only breathe slowly and shallowly when asleep.

ⓑ Explain why a trumpet player's breathing is quick and deep.

If you regularly do exercise, or play a brass instrument like the trumpet, the volume of air you breathe will probably be quite high. This is because you are used to breathing deeply and quickly. If you do little exercise, the volume of air you breathe will probably be quite low. This is because you are used to breathing slowly and shallowly. You can measure the amount of air you breathe by using a respirometer, or by using lung capacity bags.

How does cigarette smoke affect your body?

Cigarette smoke contains lots of chemicals that affect the lungs and the rest of the body. Many of the chemicals affect the oxygen supply to your body's cells. If your cells do not have enough oxygen, they will not be able to respire as much, and will release less energy. Because of this, a person may feel tired, and may get out of breath quickly when they exercise. If a pregnant mother smokes, she will reduce the oxygen supply to her baby. This can seriously affect her baby's development.

Nicotine

Nicotine is **addictive** (once you have started smoking, it is very difficult to stop). Nicotine makes your blood vessels narrower and your blood pressure higher. It also makes your heart beat more quickly, putting it under extra strain.

Carbon monoxide

Carbon monoxide cuts down the amount of oxygen the blood can carry.

Tar

Tar causes lung cancer. Cancer happens when one cell divides uncontrollably to form a tumour: a dense lump of cells. The tumour stops the lungs working properly because it uses up the space through which oxygen can go into the blood.

Tar also damages the normal air-cleaning system in our windpipe. Lining the side of the windpipe is sticky mucus, which traps dust and bacteria. Tiny hairs called cilia sweep the mucus out of the windpipe. Tar damages the cilia, so that mucus, dust and bacteria build up in the windpipe and in the lungs. The bacteria can cause infections like bronchitis.

c **Explain why people find it difficult to give up smoking, even when they know the risks to health.**

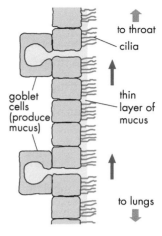

Cross-section of a normal wind-pipe

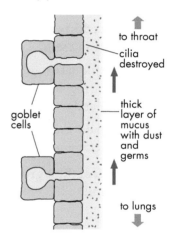

Cross-section of a damaged wind-pipe

QUESTIONS

1 Why do you breathe?

2 What happens when **a** you breathe in; **b** you breathe out?

3 Nicotine patches release nicotine into your body through the skin. Explain why using these may help smokers to give up smoking.

4 Produce a leaflet for adults explaining why smoking is harmful.

B3 # DRUGS AND ALCOHOL

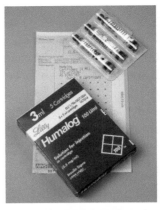

TOPIC CHECKLIST

- What is a drug?
- How do drugs affect the body?
- How does alcohol affect the body?

What is a drug?

A **drug** is a chemical that affects the way your body works.

There are three main groups of drugs.

- Medical drugs. You can buy some medical drugs simply by asking a pharmacist. For others, you need a prescription from your doctor. This is because they can be dangerous if not taken in the correct doses. Medical drugs are designed to make you better when you are ill.

- Recreational drugs. These include alcohol, nicotine and caffeine. These drugs are legal and are frequently used. Alcohol makes you happy and relaxed. Nicotine and caffeine make you feel alert.

- Illegal drugs. These include cannabis, ecstasy, heroin and amphetamines.

(a) **Which of these groups of drugs do you think is the least harmful?**

Drug	Effects
Cannabis	Relaxed feeling of happiness. May cause hallucinations. Can lead to infertility in men (unable to make sperm), bronchitis and lung cancer. May cause psychiatric problems.
Amphetamines	Alert, confident and cheerful feeling. Reduces appetite. Can cause psychiatric problems including depression and paranoia (you think everyone is out to get you!). Particularly dangerous for people with heart problems.
Ecstasy	Energetic, happy and calm feeling. May cause depression and memory loss. Inability to sleep and loss of appetite are common. Overheating while dancing can cause death.
Heroin	Warm, relaxed and contented feeling. Regular use leads to constipation (cannot go to the toilet), and reduced resistance to disease.

Fit and healthy

How do drugs affect the body?

If you take too much of any drug, it may have side effects. Side effects can permanently damage your body and affect your personality. They can even kill you. Many drugs are addictive; you may feel bad (have **withdrawal symptoms**) if you stop taking the drug.

A drug addict needs to take drugs regularly just to feel normal. Many drug addicts die from a drug's side effects before they can be helped to give up. Look at the table on the previous page to see the effects of some common illegal drugs.

How does alcohol affect the body?

Alcohol is a drug found in wine, beer and spirits. Humans have drunk alcohol for hundreds of years, but what effect does it have on the body?

People drink alcohol because it gives them a feeling of happiness and calmness. If you drink it in small quantities, this is quite pleasant, although it can have some unwanted side-effects.

- It interferes with your judgement and makes you lose your inhibitions
- It makes you lose your balance
- It makes your eyesight blurred and your speech slurred
- It makes you sleepy
- It makes you lose water
- It makes you lose heat
- It makes you react more slowly

b **Explain why you should not drink alcohol and then drive a car.**

Unfortunately, it can also have more serious effects. Alcohol is absorbed into the blood through the stomach and travels to every part of the body.

- The liver removes alcohol from the blood. However, regular drinking can lead to liver damage, and a disease called cirrhosis.
- If a pregnant mother drinks alcohol, it will travel through the placenta to the baby in her womb. This can cause foetal alcoholic syndrome, which makes babies smaller, less intelligent and disfigured.

c **Why does the government set limits on how much alcohol you should drink each week?**

QUESTIONS

1 Why do people drink alcohol and smoke cigarettes?

2 Explain the difference between a medical drug and a recreational drug.

3 a What does addictive mean? **b** What happens if you try to stop taking an addictive drug?

4 Alcohol and nicotine are legal drugs for adults. Explain why some people want to make alcohol and nicotine illegal.

B4 MOVEMENT AND EXERCISE

TOPIC CHECKLIST

- What is the job of the skeleton?
- What do muscles do?
- What can go wrong with muscles and joints?
- Are we healthier than our great-grandparents were?

What is the job of the skeleton?

Your skeleton is made of bone, which keeps your body upright and protects the organs inside your body.

ⓐ Which organs do your ribs protect?

If your skeleton were made of one single bone, you would be locked in one position. Because the skeleton is made of lots of bones, you can move almost every part of your body. The joints between bones allow them to move freely against each other.

Hinge joints allow bones to move freely backwards and forwards like a door hinge. You can find a hinge joint in your elbow.

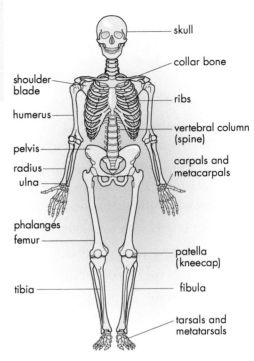

Skeleton

Ball and socket joints allow free movement in all directions. A ball on the end of your upper leg bone (femur) fits into a socket in your hip bone (pelvis). The femur can move around in any direction.

ⓑ Where else in the body can you find a ball and socket joint?

The different parts of a joint do particular jobs:

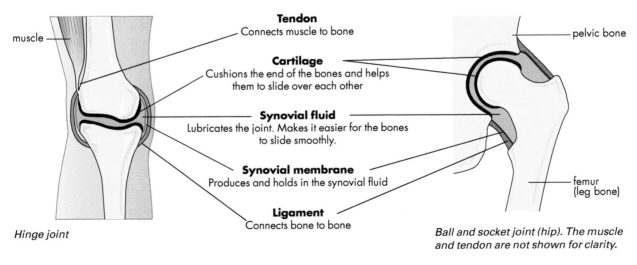

Tendon
Connects muscle to bone

Cartilage
Cushions the end of the bones and helps them to slide over each other

Synovial fluid
Lubricates the joint. Makes it easier for the bones to slide smoothly.

Synovial membrane
Produces and holds in the synovial fluid

Ligament
Connects bone to bone

Hinge joint

Ball and socket joint (hip). The muscle and tendon are not shown for clarity.

What do muscles do?

Muscles can only pull; they cannot push. There are two muscles along the upper arm: the biceps and triceps. They are both attached to the lower arm with tendons. The biceps is attached to the radius. The triceps is attached to the ulna.

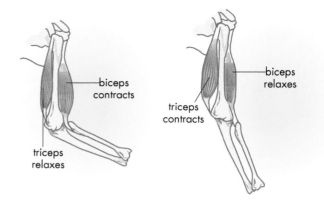

- When the biceps **contracts**, it gets shorter and fatter. This pulls on its tendon, which pulls on the radius. The lower arm lifts.

- When the triceps contracts, it gets shorter and fatter. This pulls on its tendon, which pulls on the ulna. The lower arm drops.

Muscle changes in a bent and a straight arm

When either the biceps or the triceps contracts, the other one **relaxes**. Because these two muscles pull the lower arm in opposite directions, they are called an **antagonistic pair**.

What can go wrong with muscles and joints?

Many sports injuries happen just after starting exercise. If you did not do a warm up at the start of every PE lesson, you may stretch a ligament (a **sprain**) or you may hurt a muscle (a **strain**). Both types of injury are caused by sudden or awkward movements.

c Is a *pulled muscle* a strain or a sprain?

Because athletes often put their joints under a lot of stress, the cartilage on the ends of the bones can sometimes wear away. Many old people also have problems when their joints begin to wear out. The best way to treat this is to replace the hip joint.

Are we healthier than our great-grandparents were?

You probably expect to live until you are 70 or 80 years of age. When your great-grandparents were young, people did not expect to live that long. Because people nowadays know about the dangers of a bad diet, drinking, smoking and lack of exercise, many of us are now very healthy. However, because we live longer, our bodies tend to wear out more. Arthritis and faulty joints are good examples of this.

QUESTIONS

1 What is another name for your backbone?

2 What is the job of synovial fluid in a joint?

3 What is the difference between a strain and a sprain?

4 Why do muscles have to work in pairs?

Artificial hip joint

C Plants and photosynthesis

HOW DO PLANTS GROW?

> **TOPIC CHECKLIST**
>
> ● What is photosynthesis?
>
> ● How does photosynthesis work?
>
> ● What happens if you give a plant more light?

What is photosynthesis?

Since birth, you have got a lot bigger. You will continue to grow between now and becoming an adult. Plants grow as well. In Unit 7A, you saw how a tiny redwood sapling can grow into one of the tallest trees in the world.

To grow, living organisms need food. Your food comes from what you eat. But where does a plant get its food? Aristotle, a Greek philosopher two thousand years ago, thought that plants absorb all their food from the soil. If Aristotle was correct, the soil level in plant pots should eventually go down; but this does not happen. In fact, plants make their own food using a process called **photosynthesis**. This means using light (*photo*) to make (*synthesis*) food.

How does photosynthesis work?

Plants need light, water and carbon dioxide to carry out photosynthesis.

A young redwood

A fully-grown giant redwood

- We already know that photosynthesis means making food using *light*.

- You know that plants need *water*, which they absorb through their roots.

- You may know that plants take *carbon dioxide* out of the air, which they absorb through their leaves.

When plants carry out photosynthesis they produce glucose. Glucose is a sugar which plants use for energy. Plants also make oxygen during photosynthesis. You can see oxygen being produced in Canadian pondweed. Look at the experiment, which has been left running for about one week.

The plant has produced a gas which has collected in the test tube. If you put a glowing splint into the test tube, the splint re-lights. This is a positive test for oxygen.

(a) Why would it be more difficult to prove that oxygen is produced using a normal land plant?

We now know the reactants and products for photosynthesis. Using this information we can write a word equation.

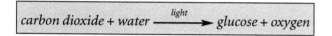

$$carbon\ dioxide + water \xrightarrow{light} glucose + oxygen$$

Light is not classed as one of the reactants because it is a form of energy. Because of this, it is put over the arrow.

What happens if you give a plant more light?

If you give a plant more light, it will photosynthesise more. Look at the pond weed in the test tubes. If you shine a light close to the pondweed, it produces lots of bubbles of oxygen. If you move the light away, it produces fewer bubbles of oxygen.

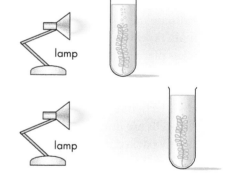

If plants photosynthesise more when there is more light, you would expect photosynthesis in a greenhouse to happen most quickly at midday, and most slowly at midnight. Becca decided to investigate this and measured the amount of oxygen in the greenhouse during the day and during the night. The graph shows her results.

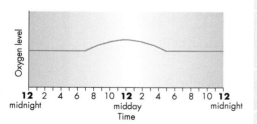

Oxygen levels in greenhouse. You should be able to see that oxygen in the air goes up during the day. This is because the plants are making the oxygen in photosynthesis.

QUESTIONS

1 What does photosynthesis mean?

2 What are
a the reactants, and
b the products of photosynthesis?

3 Why do nurses put plants into hospital wards during the day?

4 Sketch a graph showing how the amount of carbon dioxide in the air in a greenhouse changes over 24 hours.

WHAT IS THE ROLE OF THE LEAF IN PHOTOSYNTHESIS?

- How is a leaf adapted to help photosynthesis to happen?
- Why are leaves green?
- Why do leaves have different shapes in different environments?

How is a leaf adapted to help photosynthesis to happen?

Look at the leaf in the picture. It has veins and it is broad and thin. These adaptations help the leaf to get enough ingredients for photosynthesis.

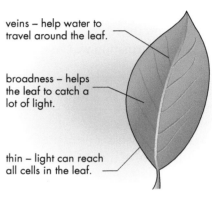

veins – help water to travel around the leaf.

broadness – helps the leaf to catch a lot of light.

thin – light can reach all cells in the leaf.

The arrangement of cells in a leaf also helps photosynthesis to happen. The leaf is made of different tissues. Each tissue is adapted to helping the leaf carry out photosynthesis. Look at the diagram to see what they are called.

- Upper epidermis – It is clear so light can pass straight through to the palisade cells beneath.

- Palisade mesophyll layer – The main layer where photosynthesis takes place. It contains chloroplasts which have a green pigment called **chlorophyll**. This absorbs light energy from the Sun. The cells are long and thin, and tightly packed near to the top of the leaf. This makes sure the maximum amount of light is absorbed.

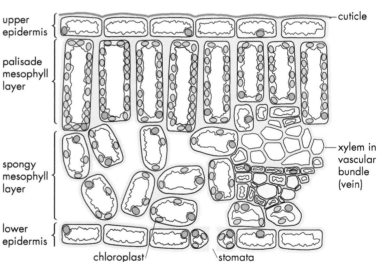

Section through a leaf

- Spongy mesophyll layer – If any light does get through the palisade layer, the spongy cells also contain chloroplasts to absorb it. The air spaces allow carbon dioxide to reach all of the mesophyll cells, and allow oxygen to escape.

- Lower epidermis – Contains tiny holes called stomata. When photosynthesis is happening, these let carbon dioxide into the leaf, and let oxygen out of the leaf.

- Xylem – these tubes carry water through the veins.

a **What is the job of the palisade layer?**

b **How is the palisade layer adapted to doing its job?**

Why are leaves green?

The green colour in leaves is caused by a pigment called chlorophyll. This catches the light energy during photosynthesis. A variegated leaf has chlorophyll in the middle, and no chlorophyll around the outside. Without chlorophyll the outside of the leaf cannot make glucose.

We can show this by testing a variegated leaf for starch. We cannot test it for glucose because a plant converts glucose to starch almost immediately after it has been made.

Parts of the leaf that contain starch will turn blue/black after the test. Look at the picture of the variegated leaf before and after being tested for starch.

Starch has only been made where chlorophyll was present, showing that chlorophyll is needed for photosynthesis.

Variegated leaf before starch test

Variegated leaf after starch test

Why do leaves have different shapes in different environments?

You may remember in Unit 7D that the shape of nettle leaves can vary. Nettles grown in the shade have very broad leaves. Nettles grown in bright sunlight have narrower leaves. The leaves are broad to absorb as much light energy as possible. Leaves in the sunlight have a good supply of light, and do not need special adaptations to absorb any more.

Photosynthesis is not the only thing that affects leaf shape. Leaves on cactus plants look like spikes. Cactus plants live in very hot places. They have spiky leaves to cut down on water loss. A narrow leaf has less **surface area** across which water can escape from the plant.

A cactus plant

QUESTIONS

1 Why is the upper epidermis clear?

2 Why are
a some leaves broad, and
b some leaves spiky?

3 An electrical company is having trouble designing its solar panels. Solar panels are made of special tiles, which make electricity when they absorb light. Using what you know about the structure of leaves, suggest what shape a solar panel needs to be to absorb light most effectively. Draw your design on a piece of paper.

WHAT HAPPENS TO GLUCOSE PRODUCED IN THE LEAVES?

TOPIC CHECKLIST

- Where does a plant get its energy?
- How is glucose stored?
- How does a plant grow and reproduce?
- How is biomass useful?

Where does a plant get its energy?

We know that plants make glucose from carbon dioxide and water in a process called photosynthesis. This process needs light energy, which is converted into **chemical energy** in the form of glucose, during the reaction.

$$carbon\ dioxide + water \xrightarrow[chlorophyll]{light\ energy} glucose + oxygen$$

You may also remember that humans use glucose in a process called respiration. Respiration releases energy from the glucose in the food we eat. This is the word equation for respiration.

$$glucose + oxygen \xrightarrow{\quad\quad} carbon\ dioxide + water$$
$$\text{Chemical energy is released}$$

You may be surprised to learn that plants also respire. Just like in humans, respiration in plants releases energy from glucose. Plants use *photosynthesis* to make glucose, which is a store of chemical energy. Having done so, they *respire* to release the energy from the glucose they have made.

a **How do animals get glucose for respiration?**

b **How do plants get glucose for respiration?**

How is glucose stored?

Most glucose that is made by photosynthesis is not used immediately in respiration. Instead, it is stored in the leaves as starch. Starch is made of long chains of glucose molecules, which coil up together.

During the night, the starch may be broken down into glucose again, and moved to other parts of the plant. When it gets there, it is stored again as starch. Look at the piece of potato, which has been tested for starch. We know that starch is stored in the potato because it has gone black.

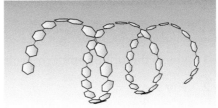

Starch is made of glucose molecules

Potato after testing for starch

How does a plant grow and reproduce?

Plants use glucose to help make other substances such as fat, sucrose, cellulose and protein. Together, these substances are used to make new cells. This makes plants bigger so that they have more mass. This extra plant material is called **biomass**. The marrow in the picture has a very large biomass. This means that it is very heavy. Biomass is measured as dry material in kilograms.

Glucose also helps to make new flowers and seeds, which helps a plant to reproduce. Some plants like carrots and onions store glucose, and then use it the following year to grow again when winter is over. They then use it to make flowers and seeds for reproduction.

Many plants store food inside their seeds. When conditions are favourable, the tiny plant inside the seed can grow, using the food for energy. Peas and beans are good examples of this kind of seed. Look at the bean in the photograph. You can see the shoot and root emerging from the bean as it germinates. They will grow using the food stored inside the bean until the leaves of the shoot start to make their own food.

C **What is a plant's biomass made from?**

How is biomass useful?

Look at the pictures to see how the different substances that make up a plant's biomass can be very useful to us.

Corn oil is made from corn plants. It contains fats.

Golden syrup is made from sugar cane. It contains sucrose.

Textured vegetable protein (TVP) comes from vegetables. Vegetarians often eat TVP to get the protein which they miss out on by not eating meat.

Wooden furniture and wooden houses are made from trees, and cotton jeans are made from cotton plants. All of them contain cellulose.

QUESTIONS

1. **a** Name three substances that make up a plant's biomass.

   b All three substances are made using one of the products of photosynthesis. Which one?

2. Why do plants photosynthesise?

3. Why do plants respire?

WHAT IS THE ROLE OF THE ROOT IN PHOTOSYNTHESIS?

TOPIC CHECKLIST

- Why do plants need water?
- How are roots adapted to absorbing water?
- How does water travel in a plant?
- Why do plants need nutrients?
- When do the roots stop working properly?

A hyacinth bulb growing roots into water

Why do plants need water?

1   Water is an ingredient in photosynthesis.

2   Water makes plants firm and upright. Plants without water wilt and go floppy.

3   Water helps plants to keep cool. Plants sweat just like you do. When the water evaporates from the plant, it takes heat energy with it.

4   Water helps to transport nutrients around the plant.

How are roots adapted to absorbing water?

Plants absorb water through their roots. Roots have a large surface area.

- Roots are branched to find new water sources. The branches increase the amount of water the roots can touch and absorb.

- Root hair cells grow outwards from the root and push into the soil. They increase the amount of water that the roots can touch and absorb.

ⓐ **Explain why roots are often branched, and have root hairs.**

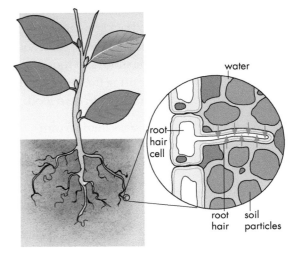

Roots absorb water and minerals and anchor the plant in the soil

How does water travel in a plant?

Once water has entered the roots, it is carried through the roots, up the stem and into the veins in the leaves. You can see the route water takes by putting a stick of celery in red dye. The red dye travels with the water up the stem and into the leaves.

By cutting across the stem of the celery, you can also see that the water only travels through certain parts of the stem. These parts are called the vascular bundles.

By examining a leaf in detail, you can see that the red ink only travels through the veins.

The veins and vascular bundles are actually collections of tubes called xylem vessels.

Why do plants need nutrients?

Plant roots not only absorb water from the soil, they also absorb nutrients. Plants need these nutrients to stay healthy.

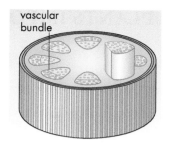 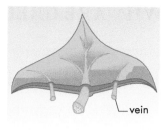

3D diagram of stem and leaf showing veins and vascular bundles

b Fertilisers provide nutrients for plants. You want to make a fertiliser to use with apple trees. Which nutrients should you include and why?

Nutrient	Nitrogen	Phosphorous	Potassium	Magnesium
Why do plants need it?	Helps to make protein, which is important for growth	Helps to make roots	Helps to make flowers	Helps to make chlorophyll
What happens to a plant that does not have enough of each nutrient?	Plant grows slowly and has small pale leaves.	Roots and stem are short, and the leaves look purple.	Few flowers or fruit are produced. Leaf edges turn yellow and brown.	Plant looks yellow or brown and cannot photosynthesise well.

When do the roots stop working properly?

If you under-water a plant, the roots cannot get any water, and they shrivel up. When they shrivel up, they stop working properly and the plant dies.

But why does a plant die if it has too much water? If you over-water a plant, there are no longer any air spaces left in the soil. Root cells respire just like the other parts of the plant. To do so, they need oxygen and glucose. Glucose is taken down to the roots from the leaves where it is made. Roots get oxygen by absorbing it from air spaces in the soil. If the roots cannot get oxygen, they cannot respire, and die.

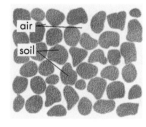

Normal soil

QUESTIONS

1 Write down three ways in which a plant uses water.

2 Which nutrient is most important for making protein?

3 Why do roots die in a water-logged soil?

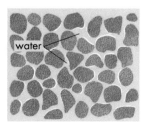

Water-logged soil

WHY ARE GREEN PLANTS IMPORTANT IN THE ENVIRONMEN'

- Why do oxygen levels in the air need to be kept constant?
- How do photosynthesis and respiration affect oxygen levels?
- Why are the rainforests important?

Why do oxygen levels in the air need to be kept constant?

Look at the graph on the right, which shows how carbon dioxide levels in the air have been increasing since 1700.

Scientists in Australia, working for the Commonwealth Scientific Industrial Research Organisation in Tasmania, have also been studying oxygen levels in the air. The graph below shows how oxygen levels have been reducing over the last 20 years.

Living things need oxygen to carry out respiration. If they cannot respire, they cannot release energy from food, and they will not survive. Because oxygen is essential for respiration, a reduction in oxygen levels could be very worrying.

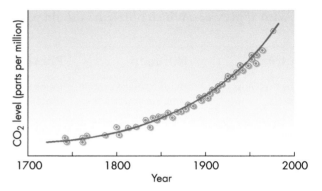

Carbon dioxide in the atmosphere, 1700 – 2000

(a) **Look at the graph of oxygen levels. How much did oxygen levels drop between 1980 and 1990?**

How do photosynthesis and respiration affect oxygen levels?

Look at the word equations for photosynthesis and respiration.

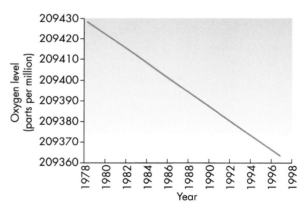

Oxygen levels in air (Courtesy of CSIRO)

- Photosynthesis uses up carbon dioxide and produces oxygen.

$$carbon\ dioxide + water \rightarrow glucose + oxygen$$
$$6CO_2 + 6H_2O \rightarrow C_6H_{12}O_6 + 6O_2$$

- Respiration uses up oxygen and produces carbon dioxide.

$$oxygen + glucose \rightarrow carbon\ dioxide + water$$
$$C_6H_{12}O_6 + 6O_2 \rightarrow 6CO_2 + 6H_2O$$

Every green plant photosynthesises. Every living organism respires. By thinking about photosynthesis and respiration, we can predict changes in atmospheric levels of oxygen and carbon dioxide.

- If photosynthesis and respiration happen at the same rate, oxygen and carbon dioxide levels in the atmosphere will stay constant.

- If respiration happens more than photosynthesis, oxygen levels will reduce and carbon dioxide levels will increase.

- If photosynthesis happens more than respiration, oxygen levels will increase and carbon dioxide levels will reduce.

The balance between photosynthesis and respiration is essential in maintaining a balance between gases in the atmosphere. You will learn more about the problems caused by increasing levels of carbon dioxide in Unit 9G.

ⓑ Write down two differences between photosynthesis and respiration.

Why are the rainforests important?

Rainforests cover a huge area of South America, Africa and Asia. Over the last 50 years, a vast number of trees in the rainforests have been cut down or 'felled'. The wood is used for making paper, furniture, or building materials. People are worried about the effect of this tree-felling on global levels of carbon dioxide and oxygen.

ⓒ If you cut down all the rainforests, what would happen to carbon dioxide levels in the air?

South American rainforest

QUESTIONS

1 Write down the word equations for photosynthesis and respiration.

2 If photosynthesis is happening more than respiration, what will happen to global oxygen levels?

3 Explain why carbon dioxide levels would be high in a greenhouse full of plants just before dawn.

4 Forests are being replanted every day across the UK. Write a short article for your local newspaper explaining the benefits of replanting.

D Plants for food

WHERE DOES OUR FOOD COME FROM?

> ### TOPIC CHECKLIST
>
> - Where do humans fit into a food web?
> - What do plants use for food?
> - Where do plants store food?
> - Why do plants store food?

Where do humans fit into a food web?

Humans eat many different animals and plants, so they are members of lots of different **food chains**. If we put some of those food chains together, we can make a very complex **food web**.

The arrows in food chains and food webs represent the flow of energy. Energy enters the food web when the plants photosynthesise using energy from the sun. Because the plants produce food using this energy, they are called **producers**.

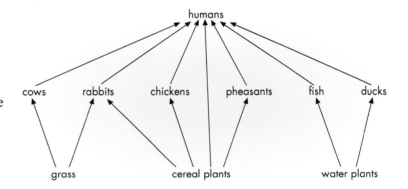

Animals cannot photosynthesise. They must get their food by eating plants or other animals. Animals are called **consumers** because they must consume their food. There are three types of consumer:

- **Herbivores** animals which only eat plants
- **Carnivores** animals which only eat animals
- **Omnivores** animals which eat both plants and animals

Cereal crops are used by humans as food

What do plants use for food?

Every living thing needs food for energy. Animals eat their food. Plants make theirs. Plants make glucose using photosynthesis:

$$carbon\ dioxide + water \xrightarrow[\text{chlorophyll}]{\text{light energy}} glucose + oxygen$$

When they need to release energy from the glucose, they use respiration:

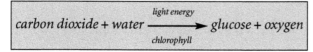

$$glucose + oxygen \xrightarrow{\hspace{1cm}} carbon\ dioxide + water$$
Chemical energy is released

ⓐ **What type of consumers are humans?**

ⓑ **What is the original supply of energy for all living things?**

Where do plants store food?

When plants make glucose in photosynthesis, they may use it straight away in respiration. They may also convert it into sucrose, starch, fat or protein and store it in particular parts of their body. Food can be stored in the roots, stem or leaves. Some food is also stored in the fruit and the seeds. You can see some examples in the photo.

Many plants store most of their food as starch. You have tested for starch before. In Unit C3 you saw that starch is stored inside a potato. If you look inside the potato's cells, you can actually see the starch grains themselves.

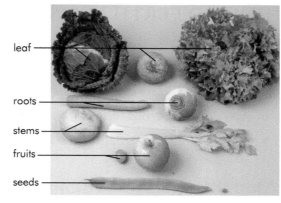

Root, stem, leaf, fruit, seed

Why do plants store food?

Plants store food for lots of different reasons. Stored food helps them to grow, reproduce and survive. We are lucky that they do so. They give us a very useful source of food.

- In the summer, there is lots of light available for photosynthesis. Plants make more glucose than they need for respiration. To stop this food being wasted, it is stored.

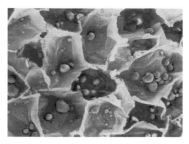

Light micrograph of starch grains inside potato cells

- Some plants store food to help them survive the winter. Food stores also give them the energy to grow again when spring arrives. Carrot plants store food in their roots during the winter. In the spring, a new stem grows out of the carrot.

- Plants store food inside their seeds, so the tiny plant inside the seed has food to help it grow.

C **In which organ does a carrot plant store food?**

Making a good food store is very important to many plants. Without their leaves, they would be unable to photosynthesise and would not be able to make any food. To protect themselves, rhubarb plants have poisonous leaves. This stops animals eating them and allows the rhubarb to store a lot of food inside its stem.

Sometimes however, plants do store food to encourage animals to eat them. To help their seeds get carried to a different location (and possibly better conditions), plants grow a fleshy sweet fruit around them. This fruit contains a store of sucrose (which tastes sweet). Animals like the taste of the fruit, and when they swallow it, they swallow the seeds as well. When the seeds leave the animal's body in its faeces, they are dropped at a new location, ready to produce new plants.

Rhubarb plant

QUESTIONS

1 Name a plant that stores its food in **a** the root, **b** the stem, and **c** the leaves.

2 Write down the word equations for photosynthesis and respiration.

3 Why is sucrose stored in fruit?

4 Give two reasons why starch is stored in roots, stems and leaves.

> ### TOPIC CHECKLIST
> - What do fertilisers contain?
> - Why do farmers use fertilisers?
> - Why do plants grow better with fertilisers?

What do fertilisers contain?

Fertilisers contain important nutrients that plants need to stay healthy. They contain nitrates and phosphates, which are salts. Nitrates contain nitrogen, and phosphates contain phosphorous. Many fertilisers also contain potassium and magnesium salts.

You can look on the label to find out which nutrients a fertiliser contains

(a)   **Why does a plant need nitrogen, phosphorous, potassium and magnesium?**

Each fertiliser always has a recommended **application rate**. This is the amount of fertiliser needed to fertilise 100 square metres of crop. Farmers can calculate how much it will cost to fertilise their crop using this information. Look at the example:

- A fertiliser comes in 5 kg bags, which cost £10 each.
- The application rate for this fertiliser is 20 kg per 100 square metres.
- The number of bags needed to fertilise 100 square metres is 20 ÷ 5 = 4.
- The cost of fertilising 100 square metres is 4 × 10 = £40.

(b)   **Mr Moore has a field of grass that is 800 square metres. How much will it cost him to fertilise this field using the same fertiliser?**

Why do farmers use fertilisers?

Using fertilisers can be very costly. The farmer must first buy the fertiliser, which is quite expensive. Then he must spend money to spread it on the fields, for example, by paying someone to drive the tractor and paying for fuel. Some farmers can save money on buying fertiliser by using manure. Manure is made of faeces produced by animals. This is often very rich in nutrients and can be spread on the fields as fertiliser.

Spreading manure

If using fertilisers is so costly, why do farmers do it? Fertilisers increase the size of each plant, so this increases the amount of crop that a farmer can harvest and sell. The extra money they receive from selling this extra crop needs to outweigh the cost of buying and spreading the fertilisers on their fields to make it worthwhile.

Why do plants grow better with fertilisers?

To be absorbed by plants, nutrients must be dissolved in water. When fertilisers are spread on fields, they may already be dissolved in water, or they may be contained in tiny solid pellets. In this case, rain will make the pellets dissolve, and the nutrients in the fertiliser will soak into the soil.

Having been absorbed into the roots through the root hairs, nutrients are transported all around the plant. Each nutrient helps the plant to grow and stay healthy in slightly different ways. The table on the right summarises what you learnt in Unit C4.

Apart from the four nutrients in the table, plants also need other nutrients in much smaller amounts. These are called **trace nutrients**. You can see what happens if a plant does not get enough of each nutrient by looking at the table below.

Nutrient	Main role in a plant
Nitrogen	Helps to make protein
	Growth of the whole plant
Potassium	Helps to make flowers
Phosphorous	Helps to make roots
Magnesium	Helps to make chlorophyll

Nutrient	What happens to a plant without enough of each nutrient
Iron	Yellow younger leaves
Copper	Leaves start to die Brown spots on leaves
Molybdenum	Narrow leaves

c Draw a plant which does not have enough of all three trace nutrients.

You can use an aquatic plant called duckweed to investigate the effect of fertilisers. Duckweed grows quite quickly by growing new leaves. By comparing the increase in the number of leaves over several weeks, you can see how different fertilisers, or different amounts of fertiliser affect growth.

QUESTIONS

1 Name four nutrients that are needed by plants.

2 What is the application rate of a fertiliser?

3 Imagine you are a magnesium atom inside a bag of fertiliser. Describe your journey from inside the bag of fertiliser to your final destination within a barley plant.

4 Marie is worried about the plants in her garden. None of them are very healthy. Write a short guide for Marie so she can work out which nutrients her plants are missing.

HOW DOES COMPETITION AFFECT PLANT GROWTH?

What are weeds?

Farmers and gardeners hate **weeds**. A weed is a plant that has started to grow where it is not wanted. There are lots of different types of weed. See if you can spot the weeds in the pictures.

Gardeners don't like weeds because they don't look very nice. Farmers don't like them because they reduce the yield of their crops. Look at the graphs showing crop yield on two neighbouring farms in England. Manor Farm grows wheat and barley. It employs people to pull up weeds every year. Oak Farm also grows wheat and barley, but does nothing about its weeds.

You can see that Manor Farm has better crop yields than Oak Farm. The difference in yield is because weeds steal resources from the crop plants.

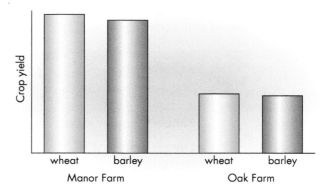

Comparison of crop yield between Manor Farm and Oak Farm

How do weeds compete for resources?

If weeds steal resources from a farmer's crop, what resources do they steal?

- The roots of weeds absorb nutrients from the soil, meaning fewer nutrients are available to the crop plants.

- The roots of weeds absorb water from the soil, so less is available to the crop plants.

- The leaves of weeds absorb carbon dioxide from the air, so less is available to the crop plants.

- The leaves of tall weeds can also absorb light before it reaches the crop.

When two plants need the same resources, we say they **compete** for resources. If two animals compete for resources they often fight. Plants cannot move, so must compete in different ways.

They may grow very tall, have broad leaves, and have widely spread and long roots. Weeds are very good at competing; they have **adapted** to competing for resources over a long period of time.

(a) Explain why being very tall helps a plant to compete for light.

(b) Explain why having widely spread and long roots helps a plant compete for water and nutrients.

How do farmers kill weeds?

On a large farm, it would be almost impossible to pull up every weed that started to grow. It would take a very long time, and need a large number of people. Farmers must make a profit from selling their crop, and the public always want to buy food as cheaply as possible. Employing more people is expensive and would increase the price of food. It is cheaper for farmers to use chemicals to kill the weeds. These chemicals are called **weed killers**.

Spraying crops with weed killer

Different weed killers contain different chemicals. Each chemical kills the weeds in a slightly different way. They may stop essential chemicals being made inside the weed, or they may make the weed grow very quickly, until it falls over and dies.

Most weed killers are selective. This means that if you spray the weed killer on a field of crops, the weed killer will have no effect on the crop plants, but will only kill the weeds.

Is killing weeds always a good idea?

Unfortunately, weed killers can have unwanted effects on food webs. Look at the food web below. This food web comes from Green Farm, which grows a lot of sugar beet. *Fat hen* is a plant that often grows in sugar beet fields.

If the farmer sprays weed killer on his crop, it will kill the fat hen plant. However, you can see that lots of birds eat fat hen seeds. By removing this source of food, fewer skylarks, pheasants and partridges will survive.

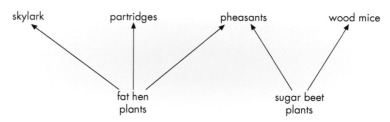

QUESTIONS

1 What is a weed?	**3** Explain why using weed killer can harm animals in the environment.
2 List four resources for which weeds compete with crop plants.	**4** Make a leaflet advertising a weed killer. Do some research to find out which chemicals you should use in your weed killer. Explain the effects of these chemicals on the weeds.

HOW DO PESTS AFFECT PLANT GROWTH?

TOPIC CHECKLIST

- What are pests?
- How do farmers kill pests?
- Is killing pests always a good idea?
- How does DDT build up in food chains?
- How does a build up of DDT affect animals?

What are pests?

Pests are animals that feed on crops grown by farmers. Pests need to find food, and crop plants are part of their food webs.

  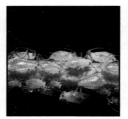  

Because the pests eat the food that is being grown for humans, they are actually competing with the humans for food. You can see this in the food web. The field mice are competing with humans for wheat and barley.

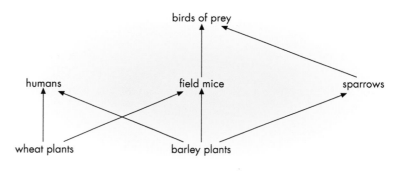

a **Using the food web, draw out two food chains containing field mice.**

How do farmers kill pests?

Farmers use chemicals called **pesticides** to kill pests and so help their crops to grow better and produce good yields.

- Insects are killed using chemicals called **insecticides**. Some (**selective insecticides**) only kill particular types of insects. Others (**non-selective insecticides**) kill any insects, even though they may not be eating the farmer's crop.

- Slugs and snails are killed using slug pellets. These pellets smell and taste nice so slugs and snails will eat them, but they contain poison so the slugs and snails will die.

Is killing pests always a good idea?

If you are a farmer and use insecticides to kill insects, you may reduce the food available to birds like blue tits and sparrows. From the pyramids of numbers, you can see that fewer blue tits can survive when there are fewer insects.

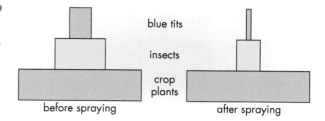

Pesticides kill animals because they contain chemicals called **toxins**. Many toxins will break down over a short period of time, so they are no longer poisonous. Other toxins do not break down, and these can cause a lot of problems in food chains.

How does DDT build up in food chains?

In 1939, a substance called DDT was invented. Scientists discovered that DDT was very good at killing insects. After the Second World War, it was used to kill mosquitoes and control the spread of malaria.

Because it does not break down easily, DDT can build up or **accumulate** in food chains. Imagine if you spray a rose bush with DDT to kill greenfly.

- Most of the greenfly would die. However, some would only absorb a little DDT. They would survive, but because DDT does not break down, it would stay in the greenflies' bodies.
- Blue tits eat greenfly. If they ate lots of greenfly, they would get lots of doses of DDT, which would build up in the blue tit's body.
- Sparrowhawks eat blue tits. Because a sparrowhawk eats lots of blue tits, it would get lots of doses of DDT, which would build up in the sparrowhawk's body.

The food pyramid shows what is happening. The total amount of DDT in each level of the pyramid is the same. However, because there are fewer individuals at the higher levels, the amount of DDT in each animal builds up. You can see how much DDT is in each animal.

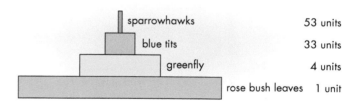

How does a build up of DDT affect animals?

DDT has not just affected sparrowhawks. Look at the food chain to see how it has built up in herons. Birds must sit on their eggs to make them warm. DDT affects birds by making their eggshells thinner. Because of this, birds affected by DDT squash their eggs when they sit on them. This was first noticed in the 1950s and 1960s as the populations of sparrowhawks, herons and cormorants fell. Since then, DDT has been banned in the UK.

QUESTIONS

1 What is a pest and who do pests compete with for food?

2 Write down two problems that pesticides can cause in food webs.

3 Explain how DDT can build up in animals high up in a food chain.

4 Explain some of the advantages of using pesticides.

WHAT IS THE PERFECT ENVIRONMENT FOR GROWING PLANTS?

TOPIC CHECKLIST

- What happens if plants do not get what they need?
- How do greenhouses help plants to grow?
- How can you farm without destroying the environment?

What happens if plants do not get what they need?

Plants need light, water, nutrients, warmth and carbon dioxide to stay healthy and survive. You can prove this by taking away each of these in turn, and observing the effects on the plant. Look back to page 27 to see the effect of depriving plants of different nutrients.

This plant has been deprived of light. It has turned very pale and grown thin and spindly.

This plant has been deprived of water. The leaves have gone dry, and the plant has gone limp and died.

This plant has been kept outside in the cold during the winter.

This plant has been deprived of carbon dioxide.

ⓐ **Why do plants find it difficult to survive without light?**

ⓑ **Give two reasons why plants find it difficult to survive without water.**

ⓒ **Give one reason why a plant needs nitrogen.**

ⓓ **Why do plants find it difficult to survive without carbon dioxide?**

How do greenhouses help plants to grow?

When you go to the florist's, you normally buy flowers that have been grown in a greenhouse. Greenhouses allow gardeners to control the light, temperature, water, nutrients and carbon dioxide available to your plants. Because the plants are isolated from the outside, a greenhouse also gets rid of competition with weeds.

A commercial greenhouse

- Light is controlled by putting shades in the greenhouse windows
- Temperature is controlled by having an automatic window that opens when it gets too hot. At night, a heater stops the temperature getting too low.
- Water is controlled automatically in commercial greenhouses using a computer-controlled system, which measures how much water is in the soil. In your own greenhouse, you decide when to water it by looking at the soil.
- The amount of nutrients is controlled by providing fertiliser when appropriate.
- Commercial growers pump carbon dioxide into greenhouses to make sure their plants are not deprived.

e **Make a list of the advantages of growing plants in a greenhouse.**

There are some disadvantages to growing plants in greenhouses. Apart from looking ugly, they are also expensive to run, and disease can spread between the plants very easily.

How can you farm without destroying the environment?

Farmers in developing countries in Africa, Asia and South America like to use modern ideas. The use of pesticides and weed killers is widespread, but there are environmental problems with using these methods of farming. It is important that farmers should farm their land in a **sustainable** way, producing their crop without destroying the environment in which they farm. So what can they do to achieve this?

1 Use bio-control. For example, greenfly can be controlled by introducing lots of ladybirds instead of using pesticides.

2 Grow plants that are more popular with insects than the crop plants. This lures insects away from the crop plant, and the farmer does not need to use insecticide.

3 Preserve hedgerows. To maximise their crop growing space, many farmers have cut down the hedges between fields, so destroying the homes of many species of birds and insects. Under pressure from environmental organisations, farmers are beginning to replant hedgerows.

4 Do not put weed killer around the edge of each field. Leave a field fallow, then weeds can grow in these areas. This provides particular animals with a food supply.

5 Use people to remove weeds from fields rather than pesticides. Organic farmers in the UK use this method. Because they must employ more people, their food is usually more expensive.

Organic food for sale

QUESTIONS

1 Describe the perfect environment for growing plants.

2 Design a greenhouse that provides everything needed by tomato plants. Draw your design, and explain how each feature of your greenhouse helps the tomatoes to survive and grow large.

3 Make a leaflet about organic farming. Find out how farmers avoid using pesticides and herbicides, and why they think their methods are good for the environment.

E Reactions of metals and metal compounds

WHY ARE METALS USEFUL?

TOPIC CHECKLIST

● What are metals?

● When is a metal not a metal?

● What are metals used for?

Potassium

What are metals?

Metals are defined by their properties – how they look and behave. The table below shows the physical properties of metals. Most metals have most of the properties in the list below, but some metals don't have all the properties, and some metals have very few of the properties.

Sodium   *Lead*

Property: metals are …	Meaning
Strong	How difficult or easy it is to break a substance: (i) by stretching (tensile strength), and (ii) by crushing (compressive strength)
Shiny and silver	Clean, fresh metal samples are reflective, and most are silver coloured
Hard	Difficult to scratch with a nail
Flexible	Bends without breaking; not rigid
Dense	Most have a lot of mass per unit volume (are heavy for their size), but some, like aluminium, are not very dense
Tough	Do not break easily when hit. Opposite of brittle
Solid	They are not liquids or gases
Good thermal conductors	Allow heat to pass through them easily
Good electrical conductors	Allow electricity to pass through them easily

When is a metal not a metal?

There are always exceptions. Mercury is a metal, but it is a liquid, so it isn't hard, strong or tough. Mercury is not the only metal with a low melting point, for example, gallium melts at 29 °C. Most metals have melting points of hundreds of degrees, and tungsten melts at 3400 °C.

ⓐ Can you think of another way in which mercury will not be like most metals?

Another unusual case is graphite. Graphite is a very good electrical conductor, but it is a dull grey solid which is brittle and a poor conductor of heat. Graphite is not a metal, but it is an extremely unusual non-metal, because almost no other non-metals conduct electricity.

Non-metals tend to be the opposite of metals. They tend to be weak, soft or brittle, not very dense, non-conductors of heat and electricity, and many of them are gases. To be certain whether a substance is a metal or non-metal, you need to look at the **chemical reactions** of the substance as well. If the substance reacts in the same way as a metal, it usually is a metal.

Graphite

What are metals used for?

Metals have thousands of uses, from making the coins in your pocket to making spaceships, cooking utensils and nuclear energy. Different metals have different properties so they are suitable for different jobs.

Aluminium cables

- Copper is an excellent conductor of electricity, so it is used for making wires and cables to carry electricity, but it is too heavy for use in overhead power lines.

- Aluminium is used for overhead electricity cables because it is much lighter than copper and is nearly as good at conducting an electric current.

- Gold is used for the wiring in spaceships, because despite the expense, it is really important that the wires do not corrode, and gold is extremely resistant to corrosion. It is also an excellent conductor.

Uranium pellets

- Uranium pellets are used to generate nuclear energy.

- Copper and nickel are used to make all the coins we use. There is also a little zinc in the £1 and £2 coins.

- Zinc is used for protecting iron dustbins and iron ships from corroding. The zinc corrodes instead of the iron.

- Iron is a strong, hard, dense metal that is extremely cheap.

- Most of the world production of lead is used in lead-acid batteries, like the ones used in cars. Lead is very dense and quite soft.

Zinc plates on a ship

ⓑ What property of aluminium makes it a good choice for using in aeroplanes?

ⓒ Why is iron a good choice when building large structures like bridges?

An iron bridge

QUESTIONS

1 Why isn't sodium used for overhead power cables?

2 Which are better conductors of electricity, metals or non-metals?

3 Why would iron be a good choice to make a hammer head?

4 Why would lead be a poor choice to make a hammer head?

5 Make a table of the properties of metals and non-metals.

HOW DO METALS REACT WITH ACIDS?

TOPIC CHECKLIST

- Strength and concentration of acids
- Which metals react with acids?
- What is made when metals react with acids?
- How are these reactions useful?

Strength and concentration of acids

Acids have a **strength** and a **concentration**. These are two different things.

The strength of an acid is related to its pH. Some acids are strong, others are weak. The strength of an acid doesn't change. For example, hydrochloric and sulphuric acids are strong acids, but acetic acid (vinegar) and beer are weak acids.

The concentration of an acid is completely different. Acids are like orange squash: they can be **concentrated** (like squash in the bottle) or they can be **diluted** by adding water, so the concentration of an acid can change.

Which metals react with acids?

Some metals react with the dilute acids we use in the lab quite quickly but other metals react with these dilute acids very slowly.

When they are placed in dilute hydrochloric acid:

Gold does not react at all

Iron reacts very slowly

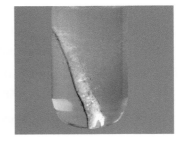
Zinc reacts quickly

What is made when metals react with acids?

When zinc reacts with sulphuric acid, we can see bubbles of gas being released. The gas is a new substance, so this is evidence that a chemical reaction is taking place. The gas released during this reaction is hydrogen.

We can prove that the gas is hydrogen by collecting the gas in a test tube and then holding a burning splint at the mouth of the tube to ignite the gas.

ⓐ **What noise does hydrogen gas make when it is tested?**

In fact, when zinc reacts with sulphuric acid two things are made. The other product is called a **salt**. We can think of a salt as 'an acid that has had its hydrogen replaced by a metal'.

The salt we put on our chips is called common salt. It is also a salt but isn't the same as the salt made here, called zinc sulphate. The salt made when zinc reacts with sulphuric acid dissolves so we can't see it. We can get a sample of the salt by evaporating the liquid in the test tube.

To understand what is happening in the reaction, we can look at the formulae for the reactants and products.

We can see that the hydrogen from the sulphuric acid is now by itself. The sulphate (SO_4) that was joined to the hydrogen is now joined to the zinc. The hydrogen in the acid has been replaced by zinc to make the salt called zinc sulphate.

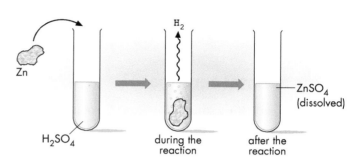

b **Magnesium reacts with sulphuric acid in a very similar way to zinc. Write the word equation for magnesium reacting with sulphuric acid.**

How are these reactions useful?

Zinc sulphate is used to help to make synthetic fibres, and in pesticides and fungicides.

Magnesium sulphate can be used in leather tanning or to 'fix' dyes.

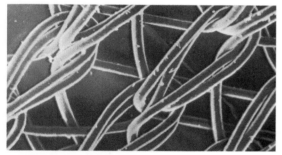

Synthetic fibres

Epsom salts

QUESTIONS

1 Name one metal that will react with most acids, and one metal that won't react with most acids.

2 Write the word equation for copper reacting with sulphuric acid.

3 Write the word equation for magnesium reacting with sulphuric acid.

4 What salt will be made when magnesium metal reacts with sulphuric acid?

5 What salt will be made when gold metal is put into sulphuric acid?

HOW DO METAL CARBONATES REACT WITH ACIDS?

TOPIC CHECKLIST

- What is a metal carbonate?
- What is made when metal carbonates react with acids?
- Which salt?
- How are these reactions useful?

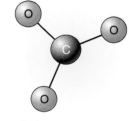

Carbonate group

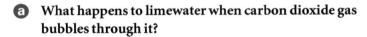

Alkalis are a sub-set of the set of bases

What is a metal carbonate?

Calcium carbonate (limestone) is an example of a metal carbonate. The metal calcium is joined to a group of atoms called a **carbonate** group. The carbonate group is made up one carbon atom joined to three oxygen atoms, so it has the formula CO_3. Metal carbonates are **bases** – the opposite of acids. Remember that bases are like alkalis: alkalis are bases that will dissolve in water.

What is made when metal carbonates react with acids?

When calcium carbonate reacts with hydrochloric acid, carbon dioxide bubbles are always released. The gas is a new substance, so this is evidence that a chemical reaction is taking place. You will have come across this reaction before when limestone is chemically weathered by acidic rainwater. We can prove that the gas is carbon dioxide by testing with limewater.

ⓐ What happens to limewater when carbon dioxide gas bubbles through it?

ⓑ What will you always *see* when an acid and a carbonate react together?

ⓒ What other evidence of a chemical reaction can you see in the photos?

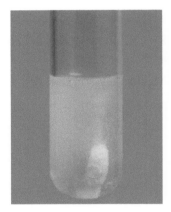

In fact, when calcium carbonate reacts with hydrochloric acid, three things are made. We already know that one of the products is carbon dioxide gas. It is given off from the carbonate group.

The second product is a salt – just the same as with metals reacting with acids. The chlorine from the acid joins with the calcium to make calcium chloride.

The third product is water. The hydrogen from the acid joins with the left-over oxygen from the carbonate group.

As all these new products are made, we know that a chemical reaction is taking place. Other evidence is that some reactions between acids and carbonates become either hot or cold as heat energy is released or taken in.

Reaction of calcium carbonate with hydrochloric acid

Whenever a metal carbonate reacts with an acid, a salt, carbon dioxide and water are made. To help you remember what happens whenever a carbonate reacts with an acid, learn this general equation:

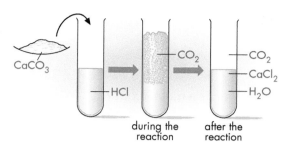

during the reaction   after the reaction

carbonate + acid → a salt + carbon dioxide + water

Which salt?

How do we know the name of the salt that has been made? This is quite straightforward as long as you know the name of the acid and the name of the substance it is reacting with. Look at the examples below.

When hydrochloric acid reacts with calcium carbonate, the CHLORI–c bit joins with the calcium to make calcium CHLORI–de.

hydrochloric acid + calcium carbonate → calcium chloride + water + carbon dioxide

When nitric acid reacts with calcium carbonate, the NITR–ic bit joins with the calcium to make calcium NITR–ate.

nitric acid + calcium carbonate → calcium nitrate + water + carbon dioxide

When sulphuric acid reacts with calcium carbonate the SULPH–uric bit joins with the calcium to make calcium SULPH–ate.

sulphuric acid + calcium carbonate → calcium sulphate + water + carbon dioxide

We can use this knowledge to make predictions about reactions that we haven't seen yet because the same thing happens when different carbonates are used. For example:

sodium carbonate + hydrochloric acid → sodium chloride + water + carbon dioxide

To help you name salts remember this:

- hydrochloric acid always makes a chloride salt
- sulphuric acid always makes a sulphate salt
- nitric acid always makes a nitrate salt.

d Write the word equation for zinc carbonate reacting with sulphuric acid.

e Write the word equation for magnesium carbonate reacting with nitric acid.

How are these reactions useful?

Calcium chloride is used to dry things and for fixing dyes. It is also used in some materials used to melt snow on roads. Calcium nitrate is used extensively in fireworks and to make football bladders. Sodium chloride is mainly used by the chemical industry to make hundreds of other chemicals, especially acids.

QUESTIONS

1 What three things are always made when an acid reacts with a carbonate?

2 Give two pieces of evidence that chemical reaction takes place between acid and a carbonate.

3 What salt will be made when any carbonate reacts with hydrochloric acid?

4 Give the names of the salts produced when zinc carbonate reacts with
a hydrochloric acid; **b** sulphuric acid; and **c** nitric acid.

What is a metal oxide?

Copper oxide is a metal oxide. It is made of copper joined to oxygen. Metal oxides are all bases – the opposites of acids. Metal oxides will react with acids following a similar pattern to that of metals and metal carbonates reacting with acids. A salt is produced.

What is made when metal oxides react with acids?

When copper oxide reacts with sulphuric acid a colour change takes place so it is likely that a chemical change has occurred. Two things are made, a salt and water. The salt is made when the copper joins with the sulphate group from the acid.

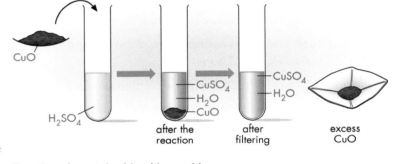

Reaction of a metal oxide with an acid

1 Reaction: A certain amount of acid is mixed with an excess of (more than enough) copper oxide, to make sure that all the acid is used up during the reaction. The mixture is stirred and heated.

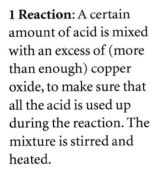

2 Filtration: when there is no more reaction, the left over (or excess) oxide is removed by filtering.

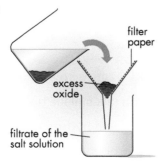

3 Separation, by evaporation and crystallisation: To separate the salt from the water it is dissolved in, about half of the water is evaporated and the solution is left to crystallise.

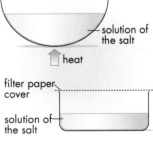

4 Product: The salt is left on the filter paper.

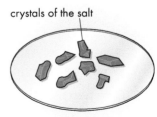

ⓐ **What would be mixed with the product if we didn't use an excess of metal oxide?**

Another way we can be sure a new product is made is by examining the product to see if its appearance is different from the appearance of the metal oxide we started with. We can also compare crystals of the product with a sample of the substance we think it is, to check our result, as crystals have characteristic shapes and colours.

We can write a word equation to show what happened:

copper oxide + sulphuric acid → copper sulphate + water

ⓑ **Write the word equation for zinc oxide reacting with sulphuric acid.**

Whenever a metal oxide reacts with an acid, a salt and water are made. Learn this general word equation:

metal oxide + acid → a salt + water

How are these reactions useful?

Copper sulphate is used to stop fungus growing on seeds and to preserve wood; tiny amounts are added to baby foods and vitamin pills.

Iron nitrate is important as a source of iron in animal feeds, and as a **catalyst** to speed up chemical processes in industry.

Calcium sulphate is also called plaster of Paris. It is used as a building material, and to clean sulphur out of smoke from burning fossil fuels.

QUESTIONS

1 Make a list of changes that would show that a chemical reaction has taken place when copper oxide reacts with an acid.

2 Explain why it is important to use an excess of copper oxide when making copper sulphate from copper oxide and sulphuric acid.

3 What does a flue gas desulphurisation plant do?

HOW DO ALKALIS REACT WITH ACIDS?

TOPIC CHECKLIST

- What are alkalis?
- Alkalis and safety
- Neutralisation
- What is made when alkalis react with acids?
- How are these reactions useful?

What are alkalis?

Alkalis are part of the group of chemicals called bases. Bases (like metal oxides) are the chemical opposite of acids. Bases that are soluble in water are called alkalis. They always have a pH number greater than 7. All metal hydroxides are bases and some of them are alkalis. Examples of alkalis include sodium hydroxide and potassium hydroxide.

All hydroxides contain a hydroxide group. This is a group of atoms that stay together. The hydroxide group consists of one oxygen atom joined to one hydrogen atom, so it has the formula 'OH'. So, all hydroxides have –OH in their chemical formulae. (This is the correct plural for formula.)

Potassium hydroxide solution

Alkalis and safety

Most people think of acids as dangerous, but they aren't as bad as alkalis. Alkalis are very good at reacting with skin and other bits of your body. They are much harder to wash off if you spill them on you. If an alkali is splashed in your eye, it will be very painful and could cause serious injury.

Neutralisation

Neutralisation is the name of the type of chemical reaction where an acid reacts with an alkali. In this type of reaction the two reactants are both used up so that the product is a neutral solution. A neutral solution has a particular pH value: pH7. This can be measured using Universal Indicator paper, Universal Indicator solution or a pH probe.

The **burette** has to be used carefully, but it can measure very small quantities of acid as they are added to the alkali. This means that we can get an accurate measurement of the amount of acid and alkali reacting to make a neutral solution.

To do this, scientists often do a 'dummy run' first, to find out approximately how much acid is needed to neutralise the alkali, and then they repeat the experiment but add the acid very slowly as they get near to the **end point** where the mixture becomes exactly neutral.

Neutralising alkali with acid

These results show the pH of the mixture as hydrochloric acid is added to 10 cm³ potassium hydroxide solution.

Amount of hydrochloric acid added/cm³	1	2	3	4	5	6	7	8	9	9.5	10	10.5	11	12	13	14	15
pH of mixture	14	14	14	14	14	14	14	14	14	12	7	2.5	1	1	1	1	1

ⓐ Draw a line graph to show the data above. The pH values should be on the *y*-axis.

ⓑ Answer these questions:
   (i) How much acid was used to neutralise 10 cm³ of the potassium hydroxide solution?
   (ii) How much acid was added to change the pH from pH14 to pH1?
   (iii) Why are the answers to (i) and (ii) different from each other?

What is made when alkalis react with acids?

When potassium hydroxide reacts with hydrochloric acid a salt is made. The potassium joins with the chloride from the acid to form potassium chloride. The hydrogen from the acid joins with the hydroxide to form water.

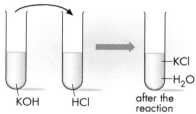

ⓒ Potassium chloride is soluble. How can we get a pure sample of it?

ⓓ Write a word equation for the reaction above.

ⓔ Write the symbol equation for the reaction above.

ⓕ What salt would be made when ammonium hydroxide is neutralised by hydrochloric acid?

Whenever an acid reacts with an alkali, a salt and water are always made. Learn this general word equation:

$$acid + alkali \rightarrow a\ salt + water$$

How are these reactions useful?

Neutralisation reactions are useful for treating insect stings, soil treatment and treating indigestion. Neutralisation reactions can also be used to make pure samples of salts such as calcium phosphate to use in washing powder or potassium nitrate to use in gunpowder.

Washing powder

QUESTIONS

1 What range of pH values shows that a substance is an alkali?

2 Explain which is safer – an acid or an alkali.

3 Write the word equation for the neutralisation of:

   a sodium hydroxide by hydrochloric acid;

   b potassium hydroxide by sulphuric acid;

   c ammonium hydroxide by nitric acid.

Gunpowder

TOPIC CHECKLIST
● Formulae make equations
● Why should equations be balanced?
● How to balance equations

Formulae make equations

We have already looked at the reaction between zinc metal and sulphuric acid (see page 43).

We can represent what happens in the reaction as a word equation:

zinc + sulphuric acid → zinc sulphate + hydrogen gas

We can also put the correct formula for each reactant and each product into an equation. This is called a **symbol equation**.

$$Zn + H_2SO_4 → ZnSO_4 + H_2$$

This equation shows how the atoms within the reactants have been rearranged to form the molecules of the products.

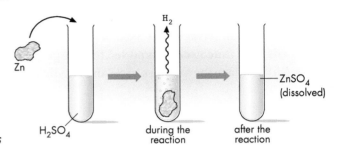

ⓐ What has the zinc joined to during the reaction?

Why should equations be balanced?

It is important to realise that there *must* always the same number of atoms in the reactants and in the products. If there are more atoms in the products than in the reactants, the equation would be saying that atoms have been created during the reaction, and this can *never* happen. If there were fewer atoms in the products than in the reactants, the equation would be saying that atoms have been destroyed during the reaction, and this, too, can *never* happen.

When we write a symbol equation we also need to make sure there are the same number of each type of atom on each side of the equation. Atoms are only rearranged in a chemical reaction.

Look at this equation for the reaction between magnesium and sulphuric acid.

magnesium + sulphuric acid → magnesium sulphate + hydrogen gas
$$Mg + H_2SO_4 → MgSO_4 + H_2$$

We can see that there are four kinds of atom involved in this reaction.

If we count up the different atoms in the reactants, we find:

Mg atoms	1
H atoms	2
S atoms	1
O atoms	4

If we count up the different atoms in the products, we find:

Mg atoms	1
H atoms	2
S atoms	1
O atoms	4

You can see that there are exactly the same number of each kind of atom on each side of the equation. As there are the same number of atoms on each side of the arrow, we say this equation is **balanced**.

ⓑ **Are these equations balanced? Count the atoms on each side of the equation as shown above to find out.**

(i) $Ca + H_2SO_4 \rightarrow CaSO_4 + H_2$ (ii) $Cu + H_2SO_4 \rightarrow CuSO_4 + H_2$ (iii) $Li + H_2SO_4 \rightarrow Li_2SO_4 + H_2$

You should have found that the first two equations are balanced, so they are correct. The third equation is not balanced, as there are more lithium (Li) atoms on the right hand side of the equation than on the left. You should not leave an equation unbalanced. So now we will look at how to balance the equation.

How to balance equations

We will use the lithium and sulphuric acid example above.

1 We start by writing the equation and adding up the number of atoms of each kind on each side of the equation:

$$Li + H_2SO_4 \rightarrow Li_2SO_4 + H_2$$

Reactants		Products	
Li atoms	1	Li atoms	2
H atoms	2	H atoms	2
S atoms	1	S atoms	1
O atoms	4	O atoms	4

2 We need to increase the number of Li atoms on the left to two. To do this, we rewrite the equation with a 'big' 2 in front of the Li, because we need two Li atoms.

$$2Li + H_2SO_4 \rightarrow Li_2SO_4 + H_2$$

3 Then we count up the atoms again.

Reactants		Products	
Li atoms	2	Li atoms	2
H atoms	2	H atoms	2
S atoms	1	S atoms	1
O atoms	4	O atoms	4

So now the equation is balanced. If it isn't balanced, repeat steps (2) and (3) by changing 'big' numbers until the equation is balanced. Remember, you can't change the subscript numbers in a formula because the formula of a compound is fixed. If you did change the formula it would become a different compound.

So there are three steps for balancing an equation:

- Write the formulae into the equation
- Add 'big' numbers in front of formulae
- Count up the atoms on each side of the equation

ⓒ **What 'big' number should be put in front of the Na to balance this equation?**

$$Na + H_2SO_4 \rightarrow Na_2SO_4 + H_2$$

ⓓ **What 'big' number should be put in front of the K to balance this equation?**

$$K + 2HCl \rightarrow 2KCl + H_2$$

ⓔ **What 'big' numbers should be added to balance this equation?** *(Hint: start by balancing the Hs)*

$$Li + HCl \rightarrow LiCl + H_2$$

QUESTIONS

1 Are these equations balanced?

  a $Mg + 2HCl \rightarrow MgCl_2 + H_2$

  b $K + HCl \rightarrow KCl + H_2$

  c $H_2 + O_2 \rightarrow H_2O$

2 Balance these equations:

  a $K + H_2SO_4 \rightarrow K_2SO_4 + H_2$

  b $Na + HCl \rightarrow NaCl + H_2$

  c $2Al + HCl \rightarrow 2AlCl_3 + H_2$

  d $Al + H_2SO_4 \rightarrow Al_2(SO_4)_3 + H_2$

Reactions of metals and metal compounds

F Patterns of reactivity

WHAT MAKES METALS CHANGE?

TOPIC CHECKLIST

- How are metals affected by air and water?
- Do metals react with oxygen?
- Which is the most reactive?

How are metals affected by air and water?

Some metals react more enthusiastically than others when they are put into acid. Do they react with the air around them at different speeds as well? Remember that air is a mixture containing oxygen and water vapour as well as many other substances.

In the photograph some of the metals are reacting with only the oxygen in the air, but most are reacting with moist oxygen – oxygen and water together. Some metals react with air as soon as they are exposed to it. When a metal loses its **lustre** – its shiny surface – we say that the metal has **tarnished**. A tarnished metal is evidence for a chemical reaction.

(a) What name do we give to the tarnishing that affects iron?

Do metals react with oxygen?

These photographs show metals changing colour. When they are freshly cut these metals are all coloured silver, but they quickly change colour as they react with oxygen in the air.

Gold does not tarnish

Iron rusts

A green tarnish on copper

Potassium at the moment of cutting

Potassium 15 seconds after cutting

Potassium 30 seconds after cutting

Sodium at the moment of cutting

Sodium 60 seconds after cutting

Lithium at the moment of cutting

Lithium 60 seconds after cutting

(b) What substance is formed when oxygen reacts with
i) potassium, ii) sodium, iii) lithium?

(c) Write a word equation for each of the above reactions.

(d) Which metal reacts fastest and which reacts slowest?

As we can see, some metals react almost instantly with the oxygen in the air, but some metals react very slowly or not at all.

(e) Look at all the photographs on the previous page. Write down one metal that reacts very slowly with oxygen and another metal that does not react at all with oxygen.

Which is the most reactive?

By comparing how the three metals, potassium, sodium, and lithium, react with oxygen we can put them in order of how quickly they react. The **most reactive** metal is the one that reacts most quickly with oxygen. The **least reactive** metal is the one that reacts slowest with oxygen. A list of substances in order of reactivity is called a **reactivity series**.

(f) Write the *most* reactive of the three metals at the top of a list above the *least* reactive metal.

Now you must put the third metal into the series. It is more reactive than the least reactive one but less reactive than the most reactive one, so it goes between the other two metals.

(g) Rewrite the reactivity series you produced in (f) to include all three metals.

The photograph of gold on the last page shows that it hasn't reacted at all, so we can put gold right at the bottom of the reactivity series. However, the photos of silver, copper and iron don't give enough evidence to allow us to put them into exactly the right place in our reactivity series. These photos *only* tell us that these metals are less reactive than potassium, sodium and lithium but more reactive than gold. So all we can do for now is to put them between gold and lithium.

(h) If you leave a piece of silver and a piece of gold in the air for the same length of time, the silver tarnishes quicker than the gold, but slower than copper or iron. Where should we place silver in our reactivity series?

QUESTIONS

1 What happens when gold is left for a long time with oxygen and water?

2 Why are potassium, sodium and lithium stored in a jar of oil rather than just in a jar?

3 Write the word equation for copper reacting with oxygen.

4 Write the symbol equation for copper reacting with oxygen. Is the equation balanced?

HOW DO METALS REACT WITH WATER?

Do metals react with cold water?

When some metals are placed in cold water, they react. Look at the photos.

When metals react with water, a gas is released. If you collect this gas in a test tube and light the gas with a splint, the gas burns with a 'popping' sound.

ⓐ What gas has been made?

The other substance produced is a metal hydroxide. Metal hydroxides are all bases, so if the metal hydroxide can dissolve in water, it is an alkali.

ⓑ What would you expect to see if Universal Indicator solution was added to a test tube containing a solution of a metal hydroxide?

Learn this general equation for when a metal reacts with water:

metal + water → metal hydroxide + hydrogen

ⓒ Write a word equation for each of the reactions taking place in the photos.

Some metals, such as magnesium, zinc, copper and iron, do not react with cold water. This is because these metals are less reactive than the ones that do react with cold water. Magnesium will not react with cold water, but it does react very slowly with hot water, because the heat provides extra energy to get the reaction going.

Potassium reacting with cold water is a very fast reaction.

Although impressive, the reaction of sodium with cold water is slower than potassium.

Lithium takes only a few minutes to react completely with cold water.

Calcium reacts quickly with cold water.

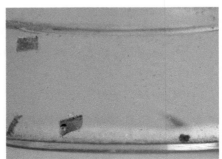

Magnesium reacts slowly with hot water

Comparing the reactivity series of metals with air and water

We have already looked at the reactions of metals with oxygen and used the information to put the metals into a reactivity series, with the most reactive metals at the top of the series and less reactive metals lower down the list.

d Use the information in the photographs on these pages to put calcium, lithium, magnesium, potassium, and sodium into a reactivity series.

e Compare the reactivity series you made for metals reacting with oxygen with the one you just made for metals reacting with water. What are the differences and the similarities?

Reactivity series for metal with oxygen	Reactivity series for metal with water
potassium	potassium
sodium	sodium
lithium	lithium
magnesium, zinc, calcium, iron, copper	calcium
silver	magnesium
gold	zinc, iron, copper
–	silver
–	gold

The metals shown in green are all less reactive than the metal above them in the list but we can't put them in order amongst themselves because we still don't have enough evidence.

QUESTIONS

1 Name one metal that reacts quickly with water.

2 Name one metal that is less reactive than zinc.

3 Name one metal whose reactivity is between zinc and potassium.

4 Write a word equation for the reaction between magnesium and water.

5 Given that the formula for magnesium hydroxide is $Mg(OH)_2$, write the balanced symbol equation for the reaction between magnesium and water.

6 Caesium is a metal that reacts with water even more violently than potassium. Where would you put caesium in the reactivity series?

F3 DO ALL METALS REACT WITH ACIDS?

TOPIC CHECKLIST

- What is formed when metals react with acids?
- Do all metals react in the same way?
- Comparing the reactivity series of metals with water and acids

What is formed when metals react with acids?

When a metal reacts with an acid, hydrogen gas and a salt are always formed.

(a) What is the name of the salt that will be formed when a metal reacts with hydrochloric acid?

(b) Write the word equation for the reaction between magnesium and nitric acid.

As we have already seen in this unit, some metals are more reactive than others. This is true for metals reacting with acids too, as you can see in the photos below.

Do all metals react in the same way?

We already know that metals have different reactivities. They will also react in different ways with acids. Some react violently and rapidly, others react slowly and some metals do not react at all. Look at these metals reacting with dilute hydrochloric acid:

Magnesium in hydrochloric acid

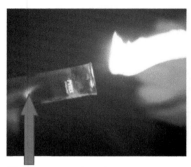

Hydrogen gas burning

Calcium

Magnesium

Zinc

Iron

In year 7 we saw that reactions of metals with acid produced hydrogen bubbles at different speeds, and also that some of these reactions generate heat. This heat is particularly noticeable if you touch a test tube of calcium or magnesium reacting with the dilute acid.

(c) Use the evidence in the four photos above to write them in a reactivity series.

Comparing the reactivity series of metals with water and acids

The order of reactivity of metals with acids is almost exactly the same as for metals with water. The order you probably came up with is shown on the right:

If you look back and compare this with the series for water or oxygen, you can see that we now have more evidence. We can use this new evidence to put the metals which were unreactive with water or oxygen into the correct places in the reactivity series.

Zinc and iron did not appear to react with water at all, although we know that given enough time iron will rust in cold water. We can now put these two metals in order below magnesium.

There are one or two metals that don't react with acids in the way that they should according to their places in the reactivity series.

When the very reactive metal calcium reacts with sulphuric acid the reaction stops after a few seconds. This is because calcium sulphate formed during the reaction does not dissolve very well in water, so instead of being carried away from the calcium it builds up a layer of the salt on the surface. This prevents any more sulphuric acid from getting to the calcium to react, so the reaction stops.

Reactivity series for metals with acid
calcium
magnesium
zinc
iron

Calcium reacts with sulphuric acid

Aluminium is a very reactive metal which goes into the reactivity series between magnesium and zinc, but often gives odd results when tested in the laboratory. This happens because the aluminium is reactive enough to form a layer of aluminium oxide all over the surface of the metal when it is exposed to air for a very short time. Very few chemicals can get through the oxide layer to react with the metal, so the only way to see aluminium react as quickly as it should is to clean the oxide layer off the surface immediately before it reacts.

acid cannot reach the calcium to react with it.

calcium atoms

calcium sulphate layer

QUESTIONS

1 Calcium metal reacts with water. How might this confuse the observations made when calcium reacts with an acid?

2 If a metal reacts slowly with an acid, does this always mean that the metal is unreactive? Use an example to help you explain your answer.

3 Write word equations for the following reactions:

 a zinc + sulphuric acid →

 b sodium + nitric acid →

 c copper + hydrochloric acid →

4 Write symbol equations for the reactions in question 3. Balance them if necessary.

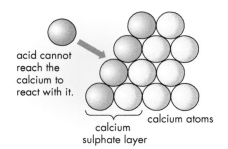

Acid (or water, or oxygen) cannot get to the aluminium atoms to react with them.

aluminium oxide layer

aluminium atoms

CAN METALS DISPLACE EACH OTHER?

TOPIC CHECKLIST

- What is displacement?
- Gathering evidence for displacement
- Creating a reactivity series
- A final reactivity series
- Are displacement reactions useful?

Zinc reacts with iron sulphate solution

What is displacement?

Displacement means 'to move from one place to another', but in science displacement means that one chemical has moved (or pushed out) another chemical out of one of its compounds. This happens to metals and their compounds. For example, when zinc metal is put into iron sulphate solution, the zinc pushes out the iron, making zinc sulphate solution. We say that the zinc has *displaced* the iron.

In displacement reactions, one of the metals must be 'stronger' than the other in some way. This is what we call reactivity. A more reactive metal can displace (or push out) a less reactive metal from a compound.

ⓐ What evidence is there in the photographs above to show that a chemical reaction has taken place?

Zinc can 'pull' the sulphate with greater force than iron, so zinc can take the sulphate away from the iron

Gathering evidence for displacement

To find out if displacement will happen we put a piece of one metal into a solution of a compound of another metal. Then we look for signs of a chemical reaction taking place, such as a colour change, a temperature change or fizzing.

The results from experiments using pairs of metals can give us information that tells us which of a pair of metals is the most reactive. To see how this works, look at the photographs below.

We can see from photograph 1 that iron reacts with copper sulphate – iron is displacing copper from the copper sulphate solution. In photograph 2 copper is not reacting with iron sulphate, so we conclude that copper cannot displace iron.

ⓑ Which metal is more reactive, iron or copper?

In photograph 3 we can see that magnesium reacts with iron sulphate – magnesium is displacing iron from the iron sulphate.

ⓒ Compare photographs 3 and 4. Which metal is more reactive, iron or magnesium?

1. Iron in copper sulphate solution

2. Copper in iron sulphate solution

3. Magnesium in iron sulphate solution

4. Iron in magnesium sulphate solution

Creating a reactivity series

Now we can use our results from the four experiments to work out a reactivity series for the three metals. The evidence from the experiments tells us that:

- iron is more reactive than copper
- magnesium is more reactive than iron;

So in order of reactivity we have:

magnesium ⟶ iron ⟶ copper

(d) **Look at the photograph of zinc reacting with iron sulphate on the opposite page. Is zinc more or less reactive than iron?**

(e) **Now look at the photograph of magnesium in zinc sulphate solution. Use your answer to question (d) and this photo to add zinc to the reactivity series.**

Magnesium in zinc sulphate solution

A final reactivity series

The extra information we get from carrying out displacement reactions allows us to add copper to our reactivity series. Bringing together all the information from this unit, we arrive at our final reactivity series (right).

Of course, this isn't the end of the story. There are other metals which we haven't put into the series here: we need to do more tests.

	Most reactive	
From metal + oxygen	potassium sodium lithium	
From metals + water	calcium magnesium	
From metals + acid	zinc iron	
From displacement reactions	copper silver	
This doesn't react at all	gold	
	Least reactive	

Are displacement reactions useful?

If a reaction is useful, it is usually because it makes a useful product. If we mix dry aluminium powder with dry iron oxide and the mixture is ignited, the aluminium takes the oxygen away from the iron oxide to make aluminium oxide and pure iron. This is an example of a displacement reaction.

Thermite reaction

aluminium + iron oxide → aluminium oxide + iron

The displaced iron is molten, and can be run into the gap between railway lines to weld them together.

QUESTIONS

1 An experiment is carried out, proving that aluminium is more reactive than iron. Why can't we use just this piece of information to put aluminium into the correct place in our reactivity series?

2 Use the reactivity series to help you complete these word equations, if any reaction takes place, and write balanced symbol equations.

   a zinc + iron chloride → ?; **b** iron + copper sulphate → ?; **c** copper + magnesium nitrate → ?

3 Write a word equation for the reaction between magnesium and iron oxide.

HOW IS REACTIVITY USEFUL?

TOPIC CHECKLIST

● How are metals found in nature?

● Can we use the reactivity series?

● How does the reactivity of a metal relate to its uses?

How are metals found in nature?

The reactivity series can help us understand how metals are found in nature. Metals are usually found in the ground, but only unreactive metals like gold and silver are found as pieces of metal. Reactive metals such as calcium, sodium and aluminium react with other elements, such as oxygen, to make chemical compounds called **minerals**.

The first metals discovered and used by people were the unreactive metals, as they were easy to find as pieces of pure metal in the ground. More reactive metals like copper were probably discovered next because they were easily extracted from their ores by heating them in air. Some metals need to be heated with charcoal (carbon) to extract them from their ores. These were discovered later, except for iron, which has been known for many thousands of years. Nearly all of the very reactive metals, which are strongly joined to other elements in their minerals, were only extracted in the last 200 years.

Gold nugget

Aluminium ore

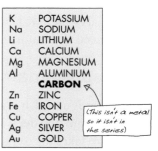

K	POTASSIUM
Na	SODIUM
Li	LITHIUM
Ca	CALCIUM
Mg	MAGNESIUM
Al	ALUMINIUM
	CARBON
Zn	ZINC
Fe	IRON
Cu	COPPER
Ag	SILVER
Au	GOLD

(This isn't a metal so it isn't in the series)

Can we use the reactivity series?

Knowing the reactivity series helps people choose the right method of extracting a metal from its ore. Look at this reactivity series.

Any metal higher in the series than where carbon is marked, such as aluminium, can only be extracted by melting the ore and then passing a large electric current through the molten mineral. This splits up the mineral, giving pure metal.

Metals such as zinc and iron, below where carbon is marked on the series, can be extracted by heating the ore mixed with carbon. The carbon joins with the other elements in the ore, such as oxygen, leaving the pure metal.

Blast furnace

Ore roasting kiln

Further down the series are fairly unreactive metals such as copper, which can be extracted from its ores just by heating in air.

@ Could we extract sodium from its mineral by heating it with carbon?

@ Could we extract copper from its mineral by heating it with carbon?

How does the reactivity of a metal relate to its uses?

Knowing the reactivity of a metal helps people choose the appropriate metal for a particular task.

Let's look at choosing a metal to use for water pipes. Gold would be an excellent choice, as it never reacts with water no matter how long it is left for or how hot the water gets.

A golden bowl

Copper is generally used today for water pipes in our homes

@ Why isn't gold used to make water pipes?

Copper would be another good choice, as it does not react with hot water.

When choosing a metal to make cutlery and food containers, silver is much better than iron. Iron can react with the water in the food, and many foods have acidic juices which would react with the iron even better than water.

@ Name one metal that would be even better than silver for making cutlery.

Metals used in jewellery are always chosen because they are unreactive, so that the metal does not tarnish. Many metals used for jewellery are expensive as well because they are rare.

@ Give one reason why iron would not make a good metal for jewellery.

The choice of metal for a purpose is not decided only on the basis of reactivity, or we might all have solid gold water pipes! But reactivity is a very important consideration when choosing a metal for a job.

Platinum jewellery

QUESTIONS

1 How would we extract zinc from a zinc-containing mineral?

2 Use your knowledge of reactivity to explain the following:

   a Gold is used for electrical wiring in satellites.

   b Iron nails last much longer when painted.

   c Lead and copper can be used as roofing materials.

   d Acid bottles are never made of magnesium.

3 "The reactivity of a metal is connected with the date when it was discovered". Say whether you agree with this statement and explain your reasons.

G Environmental chemistry

HOW ARE SOILS DIFFERENT?

Chalky soil

Sandy soil

What are the characteristics of soils?

Soils are not all the same. You can see that soils can be different colours. They can also be described using words such as, 'chalky' soil, 'sandy' soil or 'clay' soil.

Soil takes about a thousand years to form. It is made up of weathered rock fragments, plant and animal remains and animal waste. The type of soil that is formed depends on the source of the weathered rock in the soil and the amount of **organic material**, which is anything that comes from living things. The colour of the soil will depend largely on the weathered rock it is made from and the *type* of organic material in it.

Clay soil

Soils have different textures and they let water through them in different ways. Sandy soils have large grains that allow water to drain quickly through them, whereas clay soils have very fine particles that pack closely together so water cannot get through the soil easily.

Different types of soil have different pH values and contain different amounts of the nutrients that plants need to grow. You can use a soil test kit to find out the pH of a soil and how much of the main nutrients are in the soil.

A soil test kit

Which is the best soil for growing plants?

There is no such thing as the 'best' soil. Some plants prefer one soil, other plants prefer a different soil. This is one reason why some parts of the country look different to others – they have different soils so different plants grow there.

Grassy South Downs

A pine forest has no undergrowth

When you know which crops or flowers are best suited to the pH of the soil, it can help you to decide what crops to plant or how to treat the soil to suit the crops.

ⓐ **Are strawberries suited to a neutral soil?**

ⓑ **Pick one plant from the table that is unlikely to thrive in soil with a pH of 6.2.**

ⓒ **Would a cereal crop be likely to grow better in an acidic soil or an alkaline soil?**

Plant	Range of soil pH
Wheat	5.5–7.5
Barley	6.5–7.8
Oats	5.0–7.5
Potato	4.8–6.5
Strawberry	5.0–6.5
Peach	6.0–7.5
Cranberry	4.2–5.0
Broccoli	6.0–7.0

This table shows the best soil pH for growing particular plants

Can we make a soil better for growing plants?

The fact that some plants grow better in particular soils is very important to farmers. Broccoli grows best in soils with a pH in the range 6.0 to 7.0. Potatoes prefer a more acidic soil with a pH between 4.8 and 6.5.

If a farmer wants to grow broccoli and the soil is quite acidic, there are three choices:

1   grow a different crop;

2   accept that the broccoli crop will not grow well;

3   change the pH to suit the broccoli.

A typical soil in the United Kingdom has a pH of around 5, so the farmer would need to add a base to the soil to increase the pH. The most common substance used for this is called 'lime' or 'quicklime'. This is calcium oxide which is a base. It is spread on the soil.

Spreading lime to raise soil pH

ⓓ **Is a typical soil in the United Kingdom acidic or alkaline?**

ⓔ **What is the scientific name for the effect that the lime has on the acid in the soil?**

The amount of lime to add must be worked out carefully, as putting too much lime on the field costs more money and will stop the broccoli growing well. Soils in this country are rarely alkaline, but if they are too alkaline, farmers can lower the pH (the soil made more acidic) by adding peat, compost, manure or ammonium sulphate.

Muck-spreading to add nutrients and lower soil pH

QUESTIONS

1 How long does soil take to form?

2 What is soil made up of?

3 What substance can be added to soil to **a** increase and **b** decrease the pH?

4 A farmer has a big field. He takes a soil sample from the centre of the field and tests it. The soil is pH 5. Write down as many reasons as you can why this field might not be good for growing potatoes.

TOPIC CHECKLIST

- Do rocks look different as they get older?
- What makes rocks change?
- What factors affect weathering?

Weathered rocks   *Weathered statue*

Do rocks look different as they get older?

As time passes, rocks change. Rocks can change colour and shape. You can see this on buildings, monuments, gravestones, and also in natural rocks. Sometimes the change isn't obvious because you have nothing to compare the changed rock with.

a Write down how you think the statue in the photo has changed with time.

b Describe as many differences as you can between the obelisks in the two photographs on the right.

c How would you *expect* weather conditions to differ in London and Cairo?

Cleopatra's needle in London   *An Egyptian obelisk in Cairo*

What makes rocks change?

Rain and temperature are two of the main things that change rocks. The process of changing rocks is called **weathering**, which is usually a very slow process. Let's look at three types of weathering:

1 Rocks can be weathered by reacting with acidic rainwater. This is called **chemical weathering**.

d Limestone is calcium carbonate. When acidic water reacts with limestone, three substances are made. One of them is a salt. What are the other two substances made during the reaction?

e Once they have been formed, what will happen to the products of this reaction?

2 Rocks can also be weathered by changes in temperature. This is called **physical weathering**. This can be changes in the air temperature, such as in the desert, or changes in water temperature so water freezes in cracks in the rocks.

f When rocks are worn away by something rubbing against them, is this physical or chemical weathering?

Acidic water can react with limestone

g In the photograph on the right, the ground level has fallen over a period of time. Describe how the granite boulder has been weathered (i) above, and (ii) below previous ground level.

Previous ground level X – X

3 Rocks can be weathered by the action of plants or their rotting remains. This is called **biological weathering**.

It can be difficult to decide which kind of weathering is taking place where plants are growing. Roots growing through rock crevices and widening the splits in the rock as they grow is an example of physical weathering, but at the same time plants and soil tend to keep the surface of the rock moist, which encourages chemical weathering. As plants die and their remains rot away they make acidic solutions that can chemically attack rocks, especially in moist conditions. So plants cause *both* types of weathering.

h Explain how the boulder in the photograph above has been biologically weathered.

What factors affect weathering?

The weather conditions that are likely to influence the processes of weathering are:

- in hot weather chemical attack will be faster and plant growth will tend to be rapid. Rocks will expand during the day.

- in cold weather chemical attack and plant growth will be slower but ice is more likely to form at night. Rocks will contract.

- in wet weather chemical attack and plant growth are likely to be faster.

- in dry weather chemical attack will be slower and plants will not be able to grow quickly.

i Use the information from the graphs to explain why the two obelisks on page 64 have weathered differently.

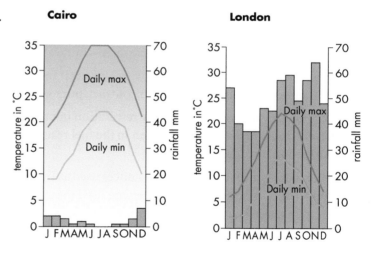

Graphs of climate for London and Cairo

QUESTIONS

1 Write down as many things as possible that can make rocks change their appearance.

2 Write down the conditions which favour:

  a chemical weathering   **b** biological weathering   **c** physical weathering.

3 Explain how plants can cause rocks to be weathered.

4 Why don't we usually notice weathering happening?

5 What types of weathering are encouraged by the weather conditions where you live?

WHAT CAUSES ACID RAIN?

TOPIC CHECKLIST

● How acidic is pure rainwater?
● What substances increase the acidity of rainwater?
● Where does the acid come from?

How acidic is pure rainwater?

As rain falls from a cloud to the ground, it passes through the air. Air is a mixture of gases. One gas that is always found naturally in pure, clean air is carbon dioxide.

As the word equation below shows, carbon dioxide is essential for **photosynthesis**. Without it, plants would be unable to make their own food. Natural processes, such as respiration in plants and animals, produce carbon dioxide which is released back into the air. The amount of carbon dioxide in the air due to respiration and photosynthesis stays fairly constant (see also Topic C1).

$$carbon\ dioxide + water \xrightarrow{\text{sunlight, chlorophyll}} glucose + oxygen$$

As rain falls, it comes into contact with the carbon dioxide, and some of the carbon dioxide reacts with the water to make an acid substance often called carbonic acid. So pure rainwater isn't the same as pure water – rainwater is a weak acid.

When samples of rainwater are tested with Universal Indicator paper or a pH probe we find that rainwater has a pH of 6. In contrast, pure water has a pH of 7.

Carbon dioxide isn't only produced by respiration in plants and animals. Whenever a fossil fuel is burned, carbon in the fuel reacts with oxygen in the air to make carbon dioxide.

All the fossil fuels and many other substances used as fuels, such as candle wax and wood, contain carbon. As fossil fuels are used to supply most of our energy and electricity, we are putting more carbon dioxide into the air every time we use energy.

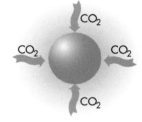

Carbon dioxide reacts with a falling raindrop

ⓐ Write the balanced symbol equation for the reaction between carbon and oxygen.

ⓑ What are the three fossil fuels?

What substances increase the acidity of rainwater?

There are other waste products from human activities that can react with rain and increase its acidity. These substances can cause harm to the environment and are called **pollutants**. The main pollutants found in air are sulphur dioxide, nitrogen monoxide and nitrogen dioxide.

Sulphur dioxide reacts with water and oxygen in the air to make sulphuric acid. Nitrogen monoxide reacts with oxygen in the air to make nitrogen dioxide that in turn reacts with water and oxygen to make nitric acid. These strong acids make the rainwater strongly acidic.

Sulphur dioxide in water: pH 3/4

So when the rain comes into contact with them, the gases react with the water making the rain more acidic than normal. They make **acid rain**, which has a pH between 2 and 5 – much lower than normal. The term acid rain only applies to rainwater that has reacted with these acidic pollutants, and is never used to refer to the normal acidity of rainwater caused by carbon dioxide.

Carbon dioxide in water: pH6

c **Write word equations for each of the three reactions mentioned in this section.**

Where does the acid come from?

Different pollutants come from different places. The diagram on the right shows the main sources of sulphur dioxide and nitrogen oxides.

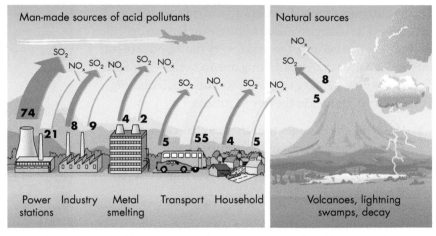

The main sources of acid gases: approximate percentages for 1998 generation of sulphur dioxide and nitrogen oxides.

- Sulphur is released into the air when fuels like coal, which usually contains up to 5% sulphur, are burned in factories or power stations. Sulphur is also released when metals in sulphide ores are smelted to produce the pure metal. During volcanic eruptions quantities of sulphur dioxide are released into the atmosphere.

- Nitrogen oxides are released when fuels burn in air, so they are produced in many factories, power stations and from car exhausts.

d **What is the main source of nitrogen oxide pollution?**

QUESTIONS

1 What is the pH of 'normal' rainwater?

2 What substance causes the rainwater to be a weak acid?

3 Name two substances that can cause acid rain.

4 How do the substances you have named in q3 get into the air?

5 A solution of water and carbon dioxide never has a pH lower than pH5, no matter how much carbon dioxide is put into the water. Could the amount of carbon dioxide in the air make any difference to the weathering caused by rainwater?

6 There are several different nitrogen oxides. Nitrogen monoxide has the formula NO and nitrogen dioxide has the formula NO_2. Why is nitrogen oxide pollution referred to as 'NO_x emissions'?

WHAT DOES ACID RAIN DO?

TOPIC CHECKLIST

- How does acid rain affect rocks and building materials?
- What are the effects of acid rain on living things?
- How can acid rain be reduced?

How does acid rain affect rocks and building materials?

The photographs show the effect of acid on some materials. The changes caused by acid rain tend to be slower than this because the acid is very dilute, but are still very much faster than weathering due to normal rainfall. This has caused damage to many monuments, including ancient Greek statues in the city of Athens.

Marble

ⓐ Describe the changes that the acid has caused in each of the materials in the photographs.

ⓑ Write the word equation for the reaction between zinc and sulphuric acid.

Lime-cemented sandstone

What are the effects of acid rain on living things?

Acid rain tends to affect plants more than animals, as animals can shelter from the rain, and have a smaller surface area in relation to their size than most plants do. Acid rain can affect plants and trees badly causing them to gradually lose leaves and eventually die. Usually the damage caused by acid pollutants takes months to have a noticeable effect.

Zinc

Acid rain can also affect fish and other organisms that live in lakes and streams by increasing the acidity of the water so much that the water plants are killed. Once this happens, there is nothing to replenish the oxygen dissolved in the water, which means there is no oxygen for fish and other aquatic life to respire. Once all the plant and animal life has decayed, the water is left sparkling clear giving the appearance of cleanliness.

ⓒ If all the young fish in a stream are killed, how could that affect (i) the population of the organisms they feed on and (ii) the population of fish in the stream over the next two years?

Acid rain damage to trees in Scandinavia

A 'dead' lake

How can acid rain be reduced?

There are many ways in which we can all help to reduce pollution and save the environment.

The diagram on page 67 shows that the major source of acid pollutants is power stations. If people and industries reduce the amount of energy they use, then there will be less acid pollution from this source. Current figures show that UK energy use is increasing by about 1% per year. Most of the increase is caused by people travelling more, and by using more energy around the house, so energy conservation at home could have a positive effect. We can also help to reduce acid pollution by using methods of transport that do not involve burning fuels in an engine, such as electric cars or even bicycles!

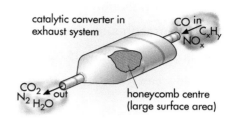

Some of the nitrogen oxides produced by car engines are removed by the use of catalytic converters, but many vehicles still do not have these fitted.

Sulphur dioxide emissions from some power stations have already been reduced by the introduction of '**Flue Gas De-sulphurisation**' plants, which are also called 'scrubbers' or 'FGD' plants. These inject powdered lime (calcium oxide) into the mixture of waste gases from the power station. The product of the reaction can be removed with a filter.

d Is lime an acid or a base?

e What kind of reaction takes place between the lime and the sulphur dioxide?

f If all power stations were fitted with FGD plants, what would happen to your electricity bill?

Some reports suggest that a number of areas in Europe are already suffering less from the effects of acid rain due to the pollution controls introduced during the last thirty years, but the problem of acid rain is far from being solved.

QUESTIONS

1 The sulphuric acid in acid rain attacks the carbonate in limestone. Write a general word equation for the reaction of sulphuric acid with a carbonate.

2 Write the balanced symbol equation for the reaction of sulphuric acid with zinc.

3 Why wouldn't magnesium be a good choice for a building material?

4 Use your knowledge of habitats and food webs to explain how acid rain damage to a forest could cause a decrease in a population of hawks living there.

5 Suggest two reasons why the amount of energy used by industry might have decreased in the last twenty years.

6 How do catalytic converters reduce the amount of polluting gases released by cars?

How is pollution monitored today?

Evidence for pollution levels in the past is readily available. For example, by looking at old photographs we can get an idea of the damage done to buildings – but this doesn't tell us when the pollution happened. We can also look at past medical records to find out if pollution-related diseases were common. Other evidence can be gained from diaries, books, newspaper reports and even the laws that were passed to clean up the environment, like the Clean Air Act of 1956 and the latest version of 1993. However, historical evidence is often hard to analyse because it isn't in the form of measurements or statistics.

Only in the last few decades have scientists started to collect numerical data about pollution so that we can plot graphs and examine trends in pollution levels. The weather is also monitored to discover the sources and method of spread of pollution.

Many pollutants are monitored, some as often as every fifteen minutes of every day of the year, using automatic sensors. Monitoring is carried out using balloons, satellites, land- and water-based sampling devices. Pollutants monitored in the UK include carbon dioxide, carbon monoxide, methane, nitrogen oxide, nitrogen dioxide, ozone and sulphur dioxide. The United Nations, the European Community and the government now monitor the environment officially. There are also schools, universities, companies and environmental campaign organisations that collect their own unofficial data.

Pollution can also be monitored by looking for **indicator organisms**. Lichens are good for this because there are many kinds of lichens and they have different tolerances to levels of acidity, so by looking at which lichens grow you can tell how polluted the environment is.

The greenhouse effect

In 1824 Jean Fourier, the French mathematician, suggested that the heat absorbed from the Sun is not all lost back into space, but some is reflected back to the surface by gases in the air around the planet. We now call this natural process the **greenhouse effect**. The main **greenhouse gases** are carbon dioxide, water vapour and methane.

a Suggest one piece of evidence that shows the environment was polluted in the past.

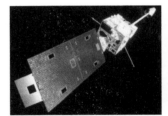

A monitoring satellite

A lichen: Teleschistes flavicans

b What would you conclude if a lichen with low tolerance of pollution was found on a tree in a city park?

Environmental chemistry

Our planet needs the greenhouse effect, because without it the *average* temperature of our world would be −18 °C rather than +15 °C. This would mean that temperatures in Britain would rarely, if ever, rise above 0 °C. However, the greenhouse effect is beginning to cause problems because scientists think that we are producing too much carbon dioxide, which will warm our planet up too much.

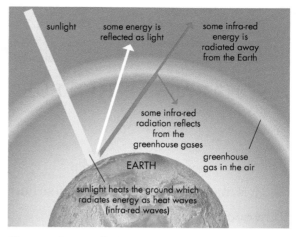

The greenhouse effect

Is global warming happening?

Global warming is the name given to the greenhouse effect going too far, so that the Earth starts heating up rather than staying at a constant temperature. If the planet warms up too much, then sea water would expand causing low-lying parts of the world to flood as the sea level rose. The changing temperature would also affect the range of living creatures that could survive. It is thought that the one class of creatures that would really benefit from global warming is the insects.

c Suggest how (i) polar bears and (ii) people might suffer as the temperatures on Earth rose.

How can we interpret the evidence?

Records show that the average temperature of the planet is climbing quite rapidly at the moment. But how should we interpret this information?

There is a great deal of evidence available but there are several problems with data.

- It is possible to create bias in the way that the data is collected, presented or used.
- There may be more than one way of interpreting what the information means.
- What you already believe could influence the way you interpret new data.
- If some of the data doesn't agree with their theory, some people may simply miss it out and hope no-one notices.

Two international conferences on global warming have been held in the last four years, in Kyoto and Buenos Aires. Eventually, an agreement was reached to reduce the amounts of greenhouse gases that countries produce, but there are still major problems to be faced. Deciding to reduce emissions is the first step. The most difficult step is going to be implementing ways of reducing the emissions.

d Can you think of one reason why a democratically elected government might not want to reduce the emissions of greenhouse gases from their country?

QUESTIONS

1 Why is it useful to measure the amounts of pollutants in the environment?

2 Name the three main 'greenhouse gases'.

3 Why are people who live on islands likely to take global warming seriously?

4 What is the difference between the 'greenhouse effect' and 'global warming'?

H Using chemistry

WHAT HAPPENS WHEN FUELS BURN?

TOPIC CHECKLIST

- What do all fuels have in common?
- What is made when a hydrocarbon fuel burns?
- How good is a fuel?
- What is made when a match burns?

Gas is dangerously flammable

What do all fuels have in common?

The word **fuel** has a very precise meaning in science. It is a substance that burns to release energy. If something releases energy without burning it is not a fuel, although it is still an energy source.

Fuels have very many different properties. They can be solids or liquids or gases. They give out different amounts of energy. Many fuels contain the elements hydrogen and carbon – these are called **hydrocarbons**.

What is made when a hydrocarbon fuel burns?

For a hydrocarbon to burn well, it needs a good supply of oxygen. When hydrogen burns, it reacts with oxygen from the air to make hydrogen oxide (water). This water is formed as a gas, water vapour, because of the heat given out by the reaction. When carbon burns, it reacts with oxygen from the air to make carbon dioxide.

For example, when methane burns in air:

methane + oxygen → water vapour + carbon dioxide
$$CH_4 + 2O_2 \rightarrow 2H_2O + CO_2$$

We can write a general word equation for when hydrocarbon fuels burn in air:

hydrocarbon fuel + oxygen → water vapour + carbon dioxide

Sometimes a hydrocarbon burns in a poor supply of oxygen. The hydrogen still burns to make water vapour. However, if there isn't enough a good supply of oxygen, then the carbon may not burn to make carbon dioxide, but instead forms carbon monoxide. Carbon monoxide is a colourless, odourless poisonous gas. Sometimes the carbon does not react with oxygen at all, and is deposited as soot.

When methane burns in a poor oxygen supply:

methane + oxygen → water vapour + carbon monoxide
$$2CH_4 + 3O_2 \rightarrow 4H_2O + 2CO$$

A general word equation for when hydrocarbon fuels burn in a poor oxygen supply is:

hydrocarbon fuel + not enough oxygen → water vapour + carbon monoxide (or carbon)

a What evidence can you get from the photograph above that gas is a fuel?

b Write the word and symbol equations for methane burning to produce water vapour and carbon dioxide.

c Why could a gas fire in someone's living room be dangerous if the room is poorly ventilated?

What is a good fuel?

There are many different features that we can use to decide if a fuel is a good one. The questions on the right will help you.

The more 'yes' answers you have, the better the fuel is. You can compare fuels by asking the same questions about each fuel.

You should also consider whether the fuel is suitable for what you want to use it for and whether it is available to you. Natural gas may be the best fuel for heating your house, but it is of no use at all when you are trying to cook your breakfast on a camping expedition in the mountains, as you are too far from the gas supply.

1 Is a lot of heat produced?
2 Is the fuel easy to light?
3 Does the fuel burn slowly?
4 Does the fuel keep burning?
5 Is the fuel easily available?
6 Is the fuel easy to store?
7 Is the fuel easy to transport?
8 Is little or no smoke produced?
9 Is little or no ash left behind?
10 Is the fuel safe?
11 Is the fuel cheap?

d Answer as many of the questions above as you can for gas, petrol and coal. Which of the three fuels gets the most 'yes' answers?

Petrol burning

Coal burning

Most people would rate gas as a 'good' fuel ... as long as it is properly controlled.

What is made when a match burns?

The 'blob' on the end of a match is usually made of a mixture of three chemicals, potassium chlorate, sulphur and carbon.

When a match is struck, the friction between the match head and the box generates enough heat energy to make the potassium chlorate decompose, giving off oxygen. The sulphur then reacts with this oxygen, making a gas which has a sharp smell.

The heat from the reaction between the sulphur and oxygen lights the carbon in the mixture which supplies enough energy to light the wooden matchstick.

QUESTIONS

1 What is a fuel?

2 What two elements are always found in a hydrocarbon fuel?

3 Why should a burning hydrocarbon fuel be given a good air supply?

4 Choose one 'good' fuel that isn't mentioned on these pages and explain why you think that it is good.

5 Explain why a match would not light if the potassium chlorate was missing from the mixture on the match head.

e Which of the substances in a match head are elements?

f What gas is made when sulphur reacts with oxygen?

TOPIC CHECKLIST

- Can chemical reactions supply energy?
- Can we make electrical energy?
- Other uses of energy from chemicals.

Can chemical reactions supply energy?

Many forms of energy can be obtained directly from chemical reactions. The main forms of energy we can get are heat energy, light energy, sound energy, electrical energy and kinetic energy.

Wood fire

Magnesium flare

Car battery

Dynamite causes explosions

Alkaline & Ni / Cd batteries

Car engine

Rocket taking off

(a) **For each photograph, write down which forms of energy are being (or could be) released.**

In Unit F we looked at displacement reactions. The thermite reaction was an example of a displacement reaction that gave out large amounts of heat and light energy. You might also have noticed that when you put pieces of one metal into a solution of the salt of another, heat energy is generated. For example, when magnesium metal is put into copper sulphate solution, the tube becomes warm to the touch, but when zinc metal is put into the same solution the temperature rise is much smaller, although still detectable with a thermometer. The further apart the metals are in the reactivity series, the more heat is generated.

(b) **Look at where magnesium and zinc are in the reactivity series. What temperature rise would you expect if iron metal is put into copper sulphate solution?**

Can we make electrical energy?

The photograph below shows how electrical energy is produced when two different metals are put into an **electrolyte** – a liquid that allows an electric current to flow through it – making a current flow between the two metals.

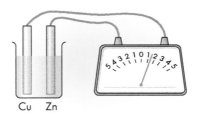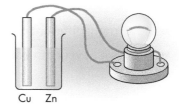

A simple voltaic cell can give electrical energy

As with displacement, different pairs of metals used in a simple cell give different voltages. The further apart the metals are in the reactivity series, the higher the voltage.

c Which simple voltaic cell would give the higher voltage, one with copper and magnesium, or one with magnesium and iron?

Other uses of energy from chemicals

The main use of chemicals in generating energy is still the burning of fossil fuels in power stations to generate electricity. Another way of producing electrical energy, called a **fuel cell**, was discovered by William Grove in 1850. It converts chemical energy directly to chemical energy. The fuel is not burnt, so it does not cause pollution. A fuel cell can run on a variety of fuels. Unlike batteries, fuel cells can be much smaller and lighter, making them more suitable for use in electric vehicles.

A great deal of work has been put into fuel cells over the last twenty years. Fuel cells have already been used successfully in the United States' space programme, and in remote buildings that need an energy supply. Around the world, companies are trying to develop them for use in vehicles and the home.

QUESTIONS

1 Write down five chemical reactions that give us the main forms of energy listed on page 74.

2 Draw a labelled diagram to show a voltaic cell illuminating a bulb.

3 Write down three ways in which chemical reactions can provide us with useful energy.

4 What advantages would a fuel cell car have over a battery powered electric car?

WHAT NEW MATERIALS CAN WE MAKE FROM CHEMICALS?

How many different materials can we produce?

The number of different chemicals we can produce is not known. There are certainly many millions of different chemical compounds, but the number increases every day, as new materials are discovered or developed. So, by the time you've written the number down, it's out of date.

The number of different chemicals that can be made *just* from crude oil is over two million. Once we include all the different materials that are made by chemical reactions in nature, the number becomes incredibly large.

Inside living things there are many different chemicals. Different proteins, fats, carbohydrates, minerals and other substances make up the tissues in our bodies. Other animals have some of the same compounds in them, but they have others as well. Plants have yet more. Each living organism can be thought of as a complicated balance of chemical reactions going on all the time – that's what keeps it alive and healthy. If the wrong chemical reactions happen in an organism, or the useful chemical reactions slow down too much or even stop, we describe the organism as unhealthy or ill.

We are very reliant on all the many new materials scientists have been able to make from chemical reactions. Some of these are shown in the photos on this page.

Chemical reactions produce all these things

a Use the information in the photographs to:
  (i) list three ways in which science directly affects our health.
  (ii) list three ways in which science affects our appearance.
  (iii) list three ways in which science affects our ability to control our environment.

b Write a word equation for a chemical reaction which only happens in plants.

How is a new chemical developed?

Some new materials have been stumbled on by accident, but today most are found as the result of a careful planning and testing process. When a new substance has been identified, it must be tested and evaluated before it can go into production. The exact details of the process can vary, but the information below will give you an idea of the main processes.

The development of a new agricultural chemical

This sequence shows the main steps in the development of a new chemical that will be used in the environment, so it is important to make sure the new substance is environmentally safe.

Agricultural worker using a new chemical

Primary screening
Laboratory testing of thousands of likely chemicals that can kill pests, weeds or harmful microbes

Data examined by registration authority
Permission given to do further tests on certain promising substances

Secondary screening
A few promising chemicals are tested further in laboratories, greenhouse trials, plot tests, field trials then large farm trials at government experimental stations.

Environmental impact assessed

Data examined by registration authority
The results of the secondary screening are checked by specialists to make sure the new chemicals do not pose a threat to the public or the environment.

Test marketing
Is there a demand for the product?

Data examined by registration authority for clearance and registration
Final checks are carried out before permission is given for the product to be put on sale.

Full scale marketing
The product is put on sale to farmers.

The development of an improved process to make a chemical

This sequence shows how a new or improved method of manufacture is gradually taken from the drawing board to a full-scale manufacturing process.

Chemical processes must be checked at every stage.

Research and development
Market research is carried out to check whether there is a demand or a need for the substance.
Market forecasts are made, estimating how much of the chemical customers might buy.
Can it be made by existing processes, or must new processes be developed?

Route selection
Which is the quickest reaction to make the substance?
Which is the most productive reaction?

Laboratory process
What apparatus is needed?
What is the best temperature to work at?
What other conditions are best?

Pilot plant process
Make a 'small factory' to make the product
Does it work well enough to make money?

Plant design and construction
Use information from the pilot plant.
Make a full scale production plant.

Plant commissioning/start-up
Get the plant ready.
Make the new product!

QUESTIONS

1 Why is it hard to say how many materials can be produced by chemical reactions?

2 Write down the names of ten useful materials that can be produced by chemical reactions.

3 When developing a new chemical process, how will the speed of the reaction affect the final price of the product?

4 Draw flow diagrams of the main stages in the development of
a a new agricultural chemical and **b** a new process to make a chemical.

WHAT HAPPENS TO ATOMS AND MOLECULES IN A CHEMICAL REACTION?

TOPIC CHECKLIST

- How are atoms rearranged?
- How much is used up?
- What about gases?
- Theory of conservation of mass

How are atoms rearranged?

During a chemical reaction, atoms in the reactants are rearranged and join together in different combinations to make new products. It is important to remember that no atoms are ever created or destroyed during a chemical reaction.

$$iron + copper\ sulphate \rightarrow iron\ sulphate + copper$$
$$Fe + CuSO_4 \rightarrow FeSO_4 + Cu$$

$$magnesium + oxygen \rightarrow magnesium\ oxide$$
$$2Mg + O_2 \rightarrow 2MgO$$

ⓐ Count the atoms in the reactants and products for each reaction. If they are the same on both sides of the equation, then no atoms have been created or destroyed.

How much is used up?

During a chemical reaction, atoms are never created or destroyed. Atoms are only rearranged during a reaction, so nothing is used up and nothing is created.

This means that if you start with 100 g of reactants, you must always end up with 100 g of product. There are no exceptions to this rule.

ⓑ **What mass of product would we get from the reaction between 112 g of iron powder and 320 g of copper sulphate solution?**

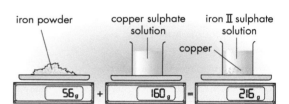

If we put 56 g of iron powder into 160 g of copper sulphate solution, we end up with 216 g of iron II sulphate solution and copper mixed together.

What about gases?

Sometimes, reactions *appear* to result in products that are heavier than the reactants. If you burn some magnesium in air, the ash after it has finished burning has more mass than the metal had at the start. Using the rule above, we know that no new atoms have been made, but some atoms must have come from somewhere, to make the magnesium heavier.

ⓒ **What does magnesium react with when it burns in air?**

ⓓ **What is the name of the substance formed when magnesium burns in air?**

Magnesium burning

When the magnesium burns, it joins with atoms of oxygen from the air to make the white powder of magnesium oxide. As magnesium has joined to oxygen, the mass has increased. The extra mass has come from oxygen.

magnesium + oxygen → magnesium oxide

$$2Mg \quad + \quad O_2 \quad \rightarrow \quad 2MgO$$
$$48\,g \quad + \quad 32\,g \quad \rightarrow \quad 80\,g$$

Sometimes reactions *appear* to result in a loss of mass. When a chemical reaction produces a gas, mass appears to be lost because the gas escapes.

When a carbonate reacts with an acid, a gas is made that turns limewater milky.

When you burn 10 g of wood, less than a gram of ash is left behind.

f **What is the name of the gas that has been made in this reaction?**

hydrochloric acid + calcium carbonate → calcium chloride + water + carbon dioxide

$$2HCl \quad + \quad CaCO_3 \quad \rightarrow \quad CaCl_2 \quad + \quad H_2O \quad + \quad CO_2$$
$$73\,g \quad + \quad 100\,g \quad \rightarrow \quad 111\,g \quad + \quad 18\,g \quad + \quad \underline{\quad}\,g$$

e **Suggest where the 'missing' atoms from the wood may have gone?**

g **The gas from the reaction above was collected and weighed. Calculate the mass of carbon dioxide that was produced.**

The theory of conservation of mass

The rule that when a reaction takes place, atoms can't be created or destroyed is called the **theory of conservation of mass**.

> **Mass is neither created nor destroyed in a chemical reaction.**

So far we have looked at the idea of conservation of mass in chemical reactions. Dissolving and changes of state are physical changes rather than chemical changes, but the rule holds for them too.

Another physical change is a **change of state**. Nothing new is being made, even though it looks very different. Nothing is added or taken away, so

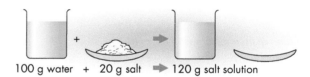

If you take 100 g of water and add 20 g of salt to the water it all dissolves and the total mass of the solution is exactly 120 g.

the mass of the substance must remain exactly the same. If we melt 100 g of ice, we must get 100 g of water. If we heat the 100 g of water until it changes to steam, we will still have 100 g, unless we let some of the steam escape.

h **If 2070 g of copper metal is melted, what mass of molten copper will be formed?**

QUESTIONS

1 What two things do not happen to the atoms involved in a chemical reaction?

2 What do the atoms involved in a chemical reaction do?

3 Explain why the mass *does* appear to increase or decrease during some reactions.

4 When a candle burns, a little of the wax melts and runs down the side of the candle. Why does a candle get so much smaller? *Hint: candle wax is a hydrocarbon.*

TOPIC CHECKLIST

● Evidence for the conservation of mass
● Checking the reliability of the experiment
● How Lavoisier proved that the theory was correct

Evidence for theory of conservation of mass

We can get some evidence to support the theory of conservation of mass by looking at the reaction of magnesium as it burns in air.

ⓐ **Write the word and symbol equations for the reaction of magnesium and oxygen.**

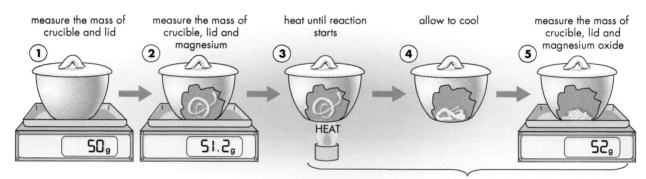

1. measure the mass of crucible and lid — 50g
2. measure the mass of crucible, lid and magnesium — 51.2g
3. heat until reaction starts — HEAT
4. allow to cool
5. measure the mass of crucible, lid and magnesium oxide — 52g

Repeat steps 3 to 5 until the same mass is obtained three times in a row.

Reaction of magnesium with oxygen

With this experiment it is hard to collect all of the magnesium oxide that is formed. When magnesium burns in air you see smoke blowing away, but the smoke is really made up of tiny particles of magnesium oxide. To get round this problem, the magnesium must be burned in a closed container such as a crucible with a lid on. We need to raise the lid occasionally to let some air in, being careful not to lose any 'smoke'.

The results shown in the diagram above indicate that mass is gained during the reaction. The mass gained is due to the oxygen that has joined to the magnesium. So, the amount of oxygen that has reacted with the particular amount of magnesium explains the difference between the mass of the magnesium at the start and the mass of the magnesium oxide that has been made.

You should only lift the lid very carefully!

ⓑ **Calculate the mass of oxygen joined to the magnesium during the reaction.**

ⓒ **Explain how this result supports the theory of conservation of mass.**

Checking the reliability of the experiment

We can carry out the experiment above using different amounts of magnesium. If all the results form a consistent pattern, they are reliable results. A scientist carrying out the experiment in the laboratory got the results below.

(d) Draw a scatter graph to show these results. Mass of magnesium goes on the horizontal axis.

(e) Draw a line of best fit through the points on your graph.

Experiment		A	B	C	D	E	F	G	H
Mass of magnesium burnt (g)		5.0	8.0	6.0	9.0	7.0	3.0	4.0	10.0
Mass of oxide produced (g)		8.3	13.3	10.0	15.0	9.2	5.0	6.7	16.7

(f) Which experiment does not fit in with the pattern?

(g) Describe the pattern in the results.

(h) Use your graph to predict how much magnesium oxide should be made from: 7 g, 2 g, 12 g of magnesium.

How Lavoisier proved the theory was correct

Antoine Lavoisier, a French scientist working in the 1700s, was one of the first to successfully apply the theory of conservation of mass in experimental chemistry.

In March 1775 he carried out a now famous experiment which took twelve days and nights. He made and then heated mercury oxide, but he was determined to find the masses of all the solids, liquids and gases involved in the reaction, using the most accurate measuring devices available. The diagrams show what Lavoisier did.

This was the first time that anyone had shown that part of the air could join onto substances. Lavoisier had also used his careful measurements to show that the theory of conservation of mass held true. Many other scientists went on to use Lavoisier's methods of finding the mass of reactants to investigate other chemical reactions. This became the foundation for all modern chemistry.

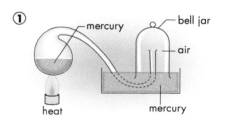

①

The mercury was heated in a flask and reacted with oxygen in the air.

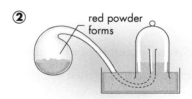

②

This made mercury oxide, using up about $\frac{1}{5}$ of the air in the apparatus.

③

When the red mercury oxide was removed and heated in a clean flask, it changed back into mercury and gave off the same amount of oxygen that had been used up in the first part of the experiment.

QUESTIONS

1 Describe the appearance of magnesium oxide.

2 When burning magnesium inside a crucible, why is it necessary to raise the lid of the crucible from time to time?

3 What mass of oxygen would react with one gram of magnesium?

4 When Lavoisier carried out the first part of his experiment, he found that 6 g of 'air' had been used up. What mass of 'gas' would he collect when he heated the mercury oxide again?

I Energy and electricity

I1 HOW IS ENERGY USEFUL FOR DOING THINGS?

TOPIC CHECKLIST

- Transfers and transformations
- How is energy stored?
- Why is electrical energy so useful?

Energy transfers from the hot liquid to the spoon

Transfers and transformations

Energy can be **transferred** from one place to another. For example, when heat is conducted along a metal spoon it moves from the spoon in the hot drink to the handle in the air.

Energy can also be **transformed** from one type to another. For example, when a fuel burns, chemical energy in the fuel is transformed into heat energy.

Energy is never lost or created, although it is sometimes difficult to see where it has gone to or come from. Energy must be transformed or transferred for anything to change in the universe. People running, aeroplanes flying, a fire burning, music playing, all involve energy changes. Here are some of the types of energy you may already be familiar with.

Chemical energy in gas is transformed into heat energy as gas burns

heat energy   light energy   sound energy   chemical energy   electrical energy

a **Give an example of a situation where each type of energy shown above is present.**

Energy is also transformed when you lift a ball up from the ground. The ball has stored energy because energy has been transformed in lifting it higher up. This energy is transformed into movement energy when the ball falls down. The energy an object has because of its height is called **gravitational potential energy**. The energy an object has because it is moving is called **kinetic energy**. When a ball falls, gravitational potential energy is transformed into kinetic energy. Springs can store energy as **potential mechanical energy**.

Sun
light energy

→

Plants
stored energy

→

Fossil fuels (petrol)
stored energy

→

Car
movement energy

Energy can be transformed quite a few times in the process of doing something. For example, to get petrol to drive our cars a number of transformations have taken place.

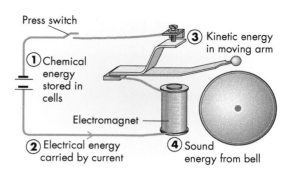

An electric bell is another good example of energy being transformed. Chemical energy in the cell is transformed into electrical energy. The electromagnets in the bell then transform the electrical energy to kinetic energy by moving a metal arm that strikes the bell. The bell itself transforms kinetic energy into sound.

How is energy stored?

Energy can be stored in all sorts of ways, for example, a book on a shelf stores gravitational potential energy, an electric cell stores chemical energy, a spring in a wind-up clock stores potential mechanical energy. When the book falls off the shelf, or electricity flows from the cell, or a clock is working, the stored energy is transformed to another type of energy that makes something happen. The energy in the book as it falls is transformed into kinetic energy. The chemical energy in the cell is converted into electrical energy. The potential mechanical energy in the spring is transformed into kinetic energy as the cogs in the clock move.

Why is electrical energy so useful?

Imagine what life would be like without electricity! Many modern devices would be impossible to use without electrical energy. Mobile phones, computers, television, microwaves and many other everyday products simply would not exist without electricity.

It is simple to transfer electrical energy from place to place along power lines supported on pylons. Electricity leaves no physical waste when we use it, whereas burning oil, coal or gas does. But you will see later that producing electricity often does create pollution.

Once electrical energy has been transferred round a circuit to a device, such as a TV, then it can be transformed easily into other types of energy, which is what makes it so useful.

d **What types of energy is electrical energy transformed into in each of these devices? (i) radio (ii) cooker (iii) electric drill (iv) TV.**

As technology improves, photo-electric cells are becoming more common. These transform light energy directly into electrical energy. Solar calculators use photo-electric cells to provide a source of energy.

Another advantage of electrical energy is the accuracy of its control. The images formed by a digital camera require very precise control of incredibly small amounts of electric current.

b **Steam engines use steam generated by heating water to move pistons. The pistons turn wheels. Identify the types of energy involved to make a steam locomotive move. Start with the coal that is burnt.**

c **Car batteries store energy and release energy when you need it. What type of energy is stored and what type of energy is produced for us to use?**

QUESTIONS

1 What is the difference between transforming and transferring energy?

2 Name a device which transforms electrical energy into movement energy.

3 Which types of energy are involved when a battery driven toy car climbs up a ramp?

4 What does a photo-electric cell do?

5 What are the advantages of an electrically powered car compared to one that runs on petrol?

6 Describe the energy transfers that take place when you watch television.

HOW DOES ELECTRICITY TRANSFER ENERGY?

- How is energy transferred in an electrical circuit?
- Where does the energy in a cell come from?
- How much push?
- High voltages are hazardous

How is energy transferred in an electrical circuit?

Electric current is the flow of electrons. Electrical energy is transferred round a circuit by the flow of current. The flow can be measured in amps using an ammeter in the circuit.

Here are some general rules to remember about current.

- Adding more cells into a series circuit makes more current flow
- Adding more bulbs into a series circuit reduces the current flow
- In a series circuit the current is the same at all points
- In a parallel circuit, the current splits when the circuit branches
- Current is not used up in a circuit, it is simply the flow of electrons through conductors in a circuit

On the right is a representation of the flow of current in a circuit as well as what is happening to the energy. Notice that the current is not 'used up'; it flows around the circuit and returns to the battery. Energy is transported by the current flow from the battery to the bulb.

Electrical energy moves around a circuit at the speed of light, so that when you press a switch on the wall, electrical energy is able to move from the power station to the light bulb in a fraction of a second.

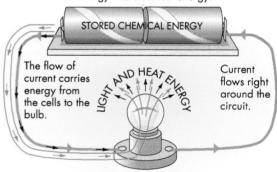

Current flows, bulb lit

More cells
More current flows, brighter bulb

More bulbs
Less current flows, bulbs dimmer

0.5 A   0.5 A   0.5 A
A series circuit current is the same all the way round.

2 A   1 A   2 A
1 A
A parallel circuit, current splits and rejoins

Cells transform chemical energy into electrical energy.

STORED CHEMICAL ENERGY

The flow of current carries energy from the cells to the bulb.

LIGHT AND HEAT ENERGY

Current flows right around the circuit.

The bulb transforms electrical energy into heat and light.

Where does the energy in a cell come from?

When the chemicals inside a cell react with each other, the chemical energy is transformed into electrical energy. The carbon rod and the zinc shell are two terminals; When the chemicals in the paste react with the zinc to provide electric current, the zinc is gradually 'eaten away'. A cell contains a large amount of energy in a small space and it is easily portable.

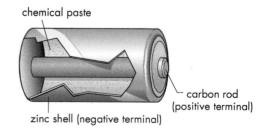

chemical paste

carbon rod (positive terminal)

zinc shell (negative terminal)

a **What evidence is there in the paragraph above that the dry cell will eventually stop providing electrical energy?**

How much push?

Cells push electric current around a circuit, this push is called the **voltage**. The voltage is measured in **volts** using a **voltmeter**. To measure the voltage in an electric circuit, we compare the voltage between two places in the circuit.

The first series circuit on the right has a cell and one bulb. To measure the voltage between one side of the cell and the other, the voltmeter is connected to either side of the cell. The voltage across the cell is 1.5 V. The second circuit contains two cells and the voltmeter reads 3 V. The higher voltage makes a larger current flow which makes the bulb glow brighter.

We can measure the voltage across the bulbs too; this is shown in the illustrations.

cell 1.5V

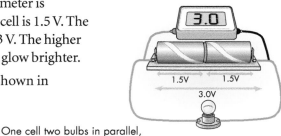
1.5V   1.5V
3.0V

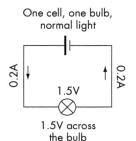
One cell, one bulb, normal light
0.2A   0.2A
1.5V
1.5V across the bulb

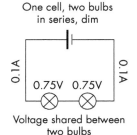
One cell, two bulbs in series, dim
0.1A   0.1A
0.75V 0.75V
Voltage shared between two bulbs
0.75V across each bulb

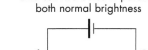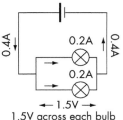
One cell two bulbs in parallel, both normal brightness
0.4A   0.2A   0.4A
0.2A
← 1.5V →
1.5V across each bulb

b Can you see a link between the voltage across the cell and that across the two bulbs?

Here are some general rules to remember about voltage.

- In series circuits, the voltage across the cells is the same as the total voltage across the other components.

- In a parallel circuit the voltage can be the same across each individual component in the circuit.

High voltages are hazardous

- The high voltages from power lines or even mains electricity in your home can kill people.

- Lightning can damage buildings and trees. Lightning conductors are placed on tall buildings to protect them from lightning strikes.

Lightning conductor

QUESTIONS

1 Looking back at the circuits above, describe what the effect would be of placing two bulbs and two cells in series.

2 Why is a cell in a radio sometimes more useful than connecting a radio into the mains?

3 Cars have batteries which contain liquid acid. Why do you think that this sort of battery is not suitable for a torch?

4 Power lines carry current at a very high voltage. Touching them with a kite or fishing line makes electricity flow through you. Explain why this is almost always fatal.

MODELS OF ELECTRICITY

TOPIC CHECKLIST

- Marble model
- Gerbil model
- How are current and voltage related?
- Is it a good model?

Marble model

- The movement of marbles represents the flow of current around the circuit.

- The paddle wheel represents a bulb which transforms the flow of marbles (current) into paddle wheel movement (light).

- The person turning the handle puts energy into the circuit. The more force the person pushes the marbles with, the more energy is carried by the flow of marbles. This represents voltage.

- As the person gets tired, they push less hard (cell running down).

This model shows us how the pushing of current at one place in the circuit, makes the current flow all the way round the circuit. It also shows us how the effect of pushing in one place is transferred immediately to all parts of the circuit.

a What happens to the paddle wheel when the person stops turning the handle? What does this represent in a real circuit?

Gerbil model

Energy is transported from one place to another in a circuit because the current flows in the circuit. We can use a different model to explain how the energy is transformed in the circuit. Imagine hundreds of wind-up toy gerbils on a track with a winding station where the gerbils are wound up to give them energy.

- As the gerbils move around the track they come to obstacles. As they manage to get past the obstacles, they lose their energy. The harder the obstacles are, the more energy they lose.

- When they get back to the winding section they have lost their energy and are wound up again.

This model shows us how some obstacles (bulbs) transform more energy than others. This energy is carried by the gerbils (electrons) moving around the circuit. The energy is not the gerbils (electrons); it is carried by them.

The clockwork gerbils transfer almost all of their energy climbing the hills.

b What do the gerbils represent?

c In the gerbil model, the winding energy comes from a person winding up the gerbils. Which part of the electrical circuit gives the electrons energy?

How are current and voltage related?

We can use the marble model to understand what happens to the current and voltage in a circuit.

- If we add another handle to the circuit, there is a larger marble flow, so the paddle wheel turns faster. In an electrical circuit this would mean the voltage is greater, the current is greater and the bulb is brighter.

- If we add a second paddle wheel into the circuit in series it is more difficult for the person to turn the handle, so the flow of marbles is smaller and the paddles turn more slowly. In an electric circuit, this would be like putting a second bulb in the circuit. The current would be less and the bulbs would be dimmer. The cell is unchanged.

- With two paddles in a parallel circuit the flow of marbles from the handle would be greater because the flow splits in two, to drive the two paddles. In an electric circuit, each bulb is the same brightness as if there was just one bulb, but the flow of current from the cell is doubled.

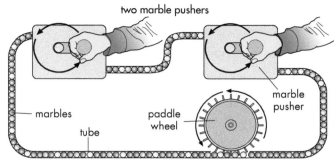

two marble pushers

marbles

tube

paddle wheel

marble pusher

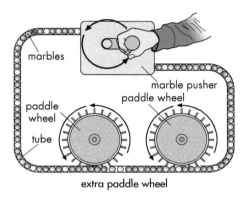

marbles

paddle wheel

tube

marble pusher
paddle wheel

extra paddle wheel

Is it a good model?

The marble model works well for current but doesn't help us imagine energy transformations. The gerbil model is better at representing the energy transformations that take place in the components of a circuit, such as a bulb. Notice also that all the energy is movement energy, in the handle or the marbles or the paddle wheels. In electrical circuits we have chemical, electrical, heat and light energy.

(d) **Think of another model for the flow of electricity around a circuit.**

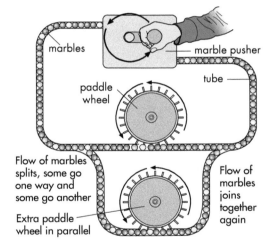

marbles

marble pusher

tube

paddle wheel

Flow of marbles splits, some go one way and some go another

Extra paddle wheel in parallel

Flow of marbles joins together again

QUESTIONS

1 Use the marble model to predict what would happen in the circuit on the right. You should mention the current flow and the bulb brightness.

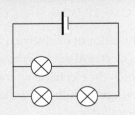

2 How would you model the filament in a bulb breaking using the marble model?

3 In a real electric circuit, the flow of electricity can be stopped by a switch, what could represent a switch in the gerbil circuit?

14

HOW DO WE USE ELECTRICITY?

TOPIC CHECKLIST

● How much energy do you use?

● How much electricity do you use?

● How can you reduce electrical energy use?

How much energy do you use?

Electric current is conducted along cables into your house. The current carries energy and transfers it to where you want to use it. The supply of electricity is called **mains electricity**. It is supplied at 240 V in the UK. This means that mains electricity can supply much more energy than a dry cell with only 1.5 V.

On a typical day you use lots of different machines that run on electricity: toaster, TV, cooker, fridge, lights, computer, iron are just some of them. Some of these devices transform more energy than others. A kettle uses over 30 times more electrical energy for the short time it is on than a light bulb would in the same time. A bulb, however, is often on for much longer.

Diane listed all of the electrical devices she used in a day and how long she used them for. She then found out the amount of energy used by each one in an hour. The unit for energy is joules (J).

ⓐ In the table below, which device uses the most energy in an hour?

ⓑ Make up a table of the different electrical devices you use each day and estimate how long you use them for.

Device	Time device used for (h)	Energy transformed per hour (J)	Total energy transformed (J)	Power rating (W)
Water heater (bath)	1	11 160 000	11 160 000	3100
Light bulb	7	360 000	2 520 000	100
Kettle	0.1	10 800 000	1 080 000	3000
Television	5	612 000	3 060 000	170
Vacuum cleaner	1	3 600 000	3 600 000	1000
Radio	2	50 400	100 800	14

How much electricity do you use?

The amount of electricity we use is measured in a slightly different way. Labels on electrical devices show the **power rating** for each device. This is the rate at which the electrical energy is transformed into another type of energy. For example, a bulb may be labelled 100 W. The table shows the power rating of various devices.

ⓒ When Diane worked out how much energy each device had transformed, she found that the vacuum cleaner had used more than the kettle, why is this?

The diagrams show the types of energy transformations that take place in the various devices.

d **Which type of energy transformation tends to need the highest power rating?**

| ❶ | electrical energy | → | heat energy | water heater |

| ❷ | electrical energy | → | light energy | |

| ❸ | electrical energy | → | heat energy | |

| ❹ | electrical energy | → | sound energy / heat energy | |

| ❺ | electrical energy | → | sound energy / kinetic energy | |

| ❻ | electrical energy | → | sound energy | |

How can you reduce electrical energy use?

We need to use less energy. The more energy we use, the more pollution we create and the worse the effects of global warming are. Using less energy helps reduce the damage we are doing to the environment. It costs less, too.

There are a number of simple changes we can make to the way we live that will dramatically reduce the amount of energy we use.

- Don't fill the kettle. Only put in as much water as you need.
- If your feet are cold, don't turn the heating up, put a pair of slippers on.
- Shut the door! Every time hot air escapes through the door, the heating system has to warm the air up again.
- Use energy efficient light bulbs. Normal light bulbs use only 10% of the energy they get to produce light. Energy efficient light bulbs use 80% of the energy to produce light.
- Switch light bulbs off when you are not in a room.
- Don't stand by. Televisions, computers, videos left on standby only use a small amount of energy each hour, but they are left on for many hours. We could shut down at least one power station in this country if everybody turned off rather than left their appliances on standby.
- Take a shower. Showers tend to use less hot water than a bath.
- Insulate. Draught excluders, cavity wall insulation, loft insulation, double glazing and carpets all help to reduce heat loss and so reduce energy use.

QUESTIONS

1 Explain why insulating a hot water tank reduces the energy you use.

2 Why would leaving the fridge door open longer than you need to cost you money?

3 Why do you think the heating bill for a detached house is larger than for a semi-detached one of similar size?

4 Energy efficient light bulbs are more expensive to buy than ordinary ones, so how do they save you money?

WHERE DO WE GET ELECTRICITY FROM?

How does a dynamo work?

A dynamo on a bicycle is one method of generating electricity. Kinetic energy in the bicycle wheel turns a wheel on the dynamo. The dynamo is a **generator**. Inside, it transforms kinetic energy into electrical energy which lights the light bulbs. The faster the bicycle is going the more electric current is generated.

How does a power station work?

Our electricity is made in power stations, which work in a similar way to the dynamo generator. Instead of a cyclist turning the bicycle wheel to turn the generator, steam is used to turn the turbine. The steam is produced by boiling water by burning fuel. Most power stations burn fossil fuels.

a **Make a list of all the types of energy being used in the power station shown.**

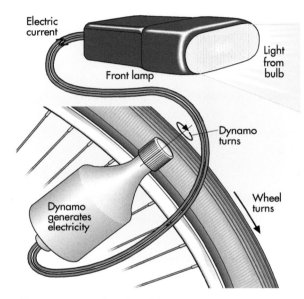

Dynamo generating electricity

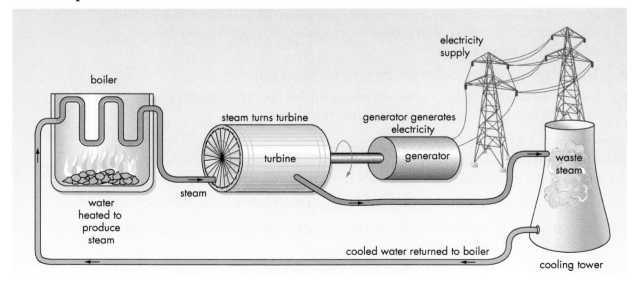

Power station

What are the problems of generating electricity?

- Power stations have to generate electricity to meet the demand for the electricity that we need at any time of the day. We usually need more during the day and less at night.

- Electrical energy cannot be stored: it has to be converted to a different form for storage.

- Coal-fired power stations cause pollution in the form of solid waste and polluting gases, but coal is widely available, fairly cheap, and easy to transport and burn.

- Generating electricity causes pollution at the point of generation, rather than where we use the electricity.

- Natural gas power stations also produce polluting gases.

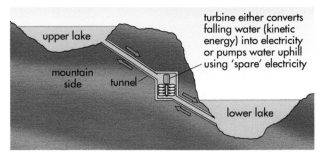

In Wales the Dinorwig lake system is used to store surplus electrical energy as gravitational potential energy. When the electrical energy is needed again, water flows back downhill driving turbines that generate electricity.

Coal, oil and gas are fossil fuels. They took hundreds of millions of years to produce and are **non-renewable fuels**. If we use them up, we will have none left for the future.

We need to reduce the amount of electricity we use:

- to conserve fossil fuels
- to reduce pollution.

ⓑ What form of energy is the gravitational potential energy of the water transformed into before it gets transformed into electrical energy?

How else can we generate electricity?

In recent years we have developed other fuels and energy resources to generate electricity. When an energy resource is used and naturally replaces itself, it is called **renewable**. Some of the examples of renewable energy from Unit 7I are listed below.

- Biomass – plants are burnt to produce heat.

- Wind energy – the energy from the movement in wind is used to turn a generator.

- Wave energy – waves make floats move up and down. This movement is used to generate electricity.

- Hydro-electric energy – falling water turns turbines which generate electricity.

ⓒ List the advantages of using these renewable energy resources.

ⓓ Are there any disadvantages of these renewable resources?

Nuclear energy is not a renewable energy source, but it is an alternative to fossil fuels. Nuclear power plants are very effective, as nuclear fuel rods contain enormous amounts of energy for their size and the power output from them is easily controlled. Although nuclear power plants do not produce greenhouse gases or smoke pollution, radioactive waste is extremely dangerous and its effects last for many centuries. Some people feel that the danger of a nuclear accident outweighs the value of their efficiency.

QUESTIONS

1 It is not possible to store electrical energy, but the Dinorwig power station stores surplus electrical energy. Explain how this is possible.

2 Electric fires are less efficient than coal fires, but people use them a lot. Why is this?

3 Why do you think that coal has been such an important fuel for electrical power generation?

WHY IS ENERGY WASTED?

- What type of energy is wasted?
- What is energy efficiency?
- What is conservation of energy?

What type of energy is wasted?

Power stations that burn fuels to generate electricity produce a lot of waste heat energy which isn't usually used. Many coal-fired power stations get rid of the waste heat using cooling towers. Waste heat is produced at all stages of the generation process.

In most energy transformations, heat energy is spread out into the air. We say the heat energy is **dissipated**. The heat is no longer useful to us.

ⓐ Look at the diagram below showing energy transformations. In what ways is energy wasted?

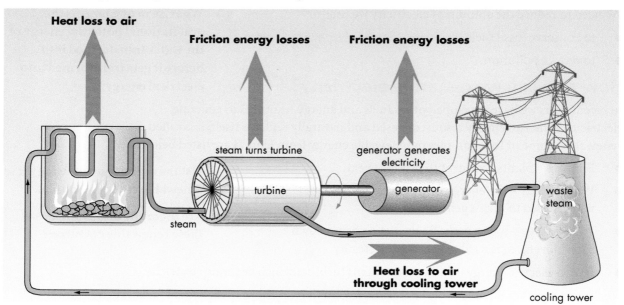

Heat loss to air

Friction energy losses

Friction energy losses

steam turns turbine

generator generates electricity

turbine

generator

waste steam

steam

Heat loss to air through cooling tower

cooling tower

Heat losses at a power station

What is energy efficiency?

By measuring how much heat energy is used, we can tell how much energy was dissipated and then work out how **efficiently** (how well) the device transforms energy.

Some electrical devices are very efficient at transforming electricity into other forms. An LED (Light Emitting Diode) is about 99% efficient. This means that for every hundred joules of energy transformed, 99 joules of light energy are produced and only 1 joule is wasted as heat energy.

Energy efficient light bulbs transform energy at an efficiency of 80% with only 20% waste heat. For years, we have used electric light bulbs with a tungsten filament. These are very inefficient, turning only 10% of electrical energy to light. The other 90% is waste heat.

b An energy efficient light bulb which transforms 11 joules each second gives out the same amount of light as a filament bulb that transforms 60 joules each second. How much energy could you save each second by using an energy efficient light bulb?

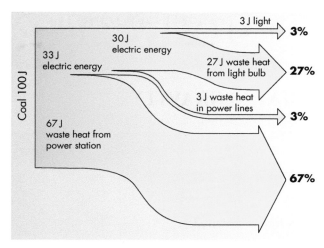

A power station can convert as little as 33% of the energy from the fuel it burns into electrical energy and 67% is dissipated as heat energy during the generation process.

If we look at the overall energy efficiency of the system, including the power stations, power lines and the filament bulb, we find that for every 100 J of energy in a bag of coal, less than 4 J of useful light energy is produced. The rest is waste heat.

Sankey diagram for a power station: from the 100 joules of chemical energy in the fuel, just 3 J ends up as useful light; 97 J is waste heat

We can use a special type of diagram to look at the energy transformation and loss at each stage. This is called a **Sankey** diagram.

What is conservation of energy?

We have looked at how heat energy is dissipated so we can't use it any more. But this doesn't mean that the energy doesn't exist any more. Energy is moved from place to place by transfers and changed from one type to another by transformations, but it is never created or destroyed. It is always conserved. This is called **conservation of energy**.

The Sankey diagram shows us that energy is conserved. All the energy that goes in at the start, ends up somewhere. It isn't lost.

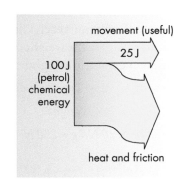

c Look at the Sankey diagram for a petrol engine. It shows the energy transformations whilst the car is driven. How much energy is wasted as heat and friction?

QUESTIONS

1 Why do you think we still use filament bulbs, if they are so inefficient?

2 Explain the difference between saving energy and 'conservation of energy'.

3 Why are you damaging the environment when you leave a light bulb on?

4 The energy diagram for a light bulb shows the heat losses. How much energy does the light bulb give out as light?

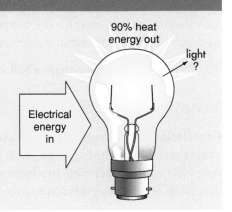

J Gravity and space

J1 WHAT IS GRAVITY?

> ### TOPIC CHECKLIST
> - Mass and weight
> - Why do things fall?
> - What is gravity?
> - How much do you weigh on the Earth?

Mass and weight

Mass is a measure of how much material you have got. If you put a brick anywhere in the universe, it will have the same mass. **Weight** is the name we give to the pull of gravity on a mass.

On Earth, a mass of 1 kg has a weight of about 10 N. The force of gravity on Earth pulls each kilogram of material with a force of 10 N. To calculate the weight of a mass on the Earth you simply multiply the mass in kilograms by 10.

A mass of 23 kg will have a weight, on the Earth, of about 230 N.

Mass × *10* = *Weight*

23 kg × *10 N/kg* = *230 N*

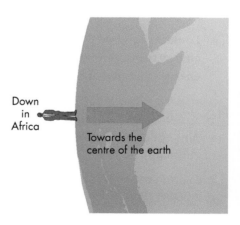

Down in the UK

Down in Australia

Why do things fall?

If you jump from a tall building, you fall downwards towards the ground. In fact, you are falling towards the centre of the Earth. When we talk about falling, then in the UK or Australia 'downwards' means 'towards the centre of the Earth'. Gravity holds us down on the Earth and stops us floating away into space.

Down in Africa

Towards the centre of the earth

ⓐ When Josh in Africa drops a ball, in which direction will it fall?

What is gravity?

Gravitation is a pulling force. It acts as an attractive force between any two masses. The two objects pull or attract each other. The bigger the mass of the object, the bigger the force the object pulls other masses with. An object with a larger mass produces a larger **gravitational force** than an object with a smaller mass. The Earth is larger so it attracts a mass more strongly than a person attracts the same mass.

ⓑ Draw a diagram with arrows showing the force of gravity on a mass of 10 kg and a mass of 30 kg near the surface of the Earth.

The scientist, Newton, based his work upon the discoveries of earlier scientists including Galileo. Anybody can observe that objects fall towards the Earth's surface. Newton's breakthrough was that he developed one simple mathematical equation which explained the movement of an apple falling from a tree and the planets moving around the Sun.

$$F = \frac{Gm_1 m_2}{r^2}$$

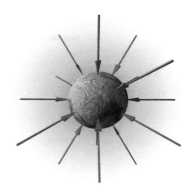

Gravitational field lines show in which direction the earth's gravitational field pulls on a mass

Around the Earth is a gravitational field which attracts any mass, including the Moon.

c **Mars has more mass than the Moon. Why is the Earth's pull on the Moon so much bigger than its pull on Mars?**

How much do you weigh on Earth?

If you ask the question 'How much do you weigh on Earth?', you are asking about the force that the Earth's gravitational field is exerting on you.

You multiply your mass by gravity to get your weight.

weight in N = mass in kg × gravity in N/kg

A person with a mass of 60 kg standing on the surface of the earth will have a weight of about 600 N.

weight = 60 kg × 10 N/kg

weight = 600 N

The Earth's gravitational field has a strength of 9.81 N/kg but we often round it up to 10 N/kg.

QUESTIONS

1 Explain the statement 'Down is in a different direction in Sydney and London.'

2 What is the weight of a 12 kg mass on the Earth?

3 Copy and complete the conversion chart on the right which shows the weight of different masses on the Earth (the first example has been done for you).

Mass	Weight
1 kg	10 N
5 kg	
	27 N
0.3 kg	
	2.7 N

HOW DOES GRAVITY CHANGE?

How much do you weigh on the Moon?

On the Moon, people weigh less than on the Earth. Their bodies have the same mass but the Moon's gravitational field is weaker than the Earth's, so they are not attracted to the Moon with so much force. When people land on the Moon, they find walking difficult because there is less gravity to hold them down on the surface of the moon, so they tend to bounce off the ground.

At its surface, the Moon's gravitational force is about one sixth of the Earth's, so the weight of an object is six times less than on Earth.

A person with a mass of 60 kg standing on the surface of the Moon will have a weight of about 100 N.

$$weight = mass \times gravitational\ field$$
$$weight = 60\ kg \times 1.7\ N/kg$$
$$weight = 102\ N$$

Mass	Weight on Moon
1 kg	1.7 N
5 kg	
2.7 kg	
0.3 kg	
0.27 kg	

a Copy and complete the conversion chart on the right which shows the weight of different masses on the Moon (the first example has been done for you).

b Walking on the moon is different from walking on the Earth. Describe how three other activities would be different or more difficult on the Moon.

Where else is gravity different?

If you went to the surface of a different planet, you would have a different weight. This is because the planets in our solar system are different sizes and masses.

Pluto has 81 times less mass than the Earth and you would weigh less on its surface. Jupiter has the biggest mass in the solar system and on its surface, you would be heaviest. On the surface of Saturn, you would weigh less than on Earth. Although Saturn has 95 times more mass, it has a much larger diameter than the Earth, so you would be much further away from the centre of the planet.

Planet	Gravitational field strength (N/kg)
Mercury	3.7
Venus	8.8
Earth	9.8
Mars	3.7
Jupiter	23.2
Saturn	9.0
Uranus	8.7
Neptune	11.1
Pluto	0.6

c Use the information on this page to calculate the weight of a person with a mass of 60 kg on each planet.

How does distance affect gravity?

We already know that an object with a bigger mass has a stronger gravitational field. But the gravitational force actually gets weaker as you get further away from the centre of an object.

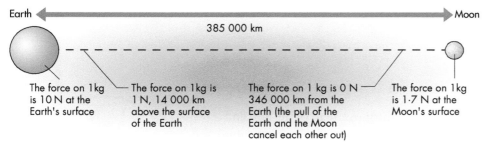

Earth ◄──────── 385 000 km ────────► Moon

The force on 1 kg is 10 N at the Earth's surface

The force on 1 kg is 1 N, 14 000 km above the surface of the Earth

The force on 1 kg is 0 N 346 000 km from the Earth (the pull of the Earth and the Moon cancel each other out)

The force on 1 kg is 1·7 N at the Moon's surface

What is the force on a mass of 1 kg?

If we think about the Earth and the Moon, then the gravitational force between them depends on their masses and the distance between them. Similarly, the gravitational force between any planet and the Sun depends on their masses and the distance between it and the Sun.

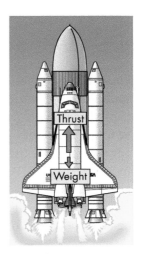

The rocket lifts off when thrust from the rocket engines is greater than its weight

(d) What happens to the weight of an apple as it is taken higher above the Earth's surface?

(e) Why don't you notice the difference in your weight when you climb some stairs?

How do rockets leave the Earth?

A rocket needs to have a lifting force (thrust) larger than its weight in order to lift off because it has to overcome the Earth's gravitational force.

As the rocket lifts into the sky there are two things that make it easier for it to escape the Earth's gravitational attraction. Firstly, the mass of the rocket decreases because it is burning fuel, so it needs less thrust, or force, as it has less mass. Secondly, the higher the rocket climbs, the weaker the gravitational attraction of the Earth becomes, so the rocket weighs less and so needs less thrust to lift it.

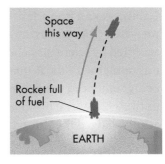

Mass of rocket decreases as fuel burns. Gravity also decreases as rocket gets higher, so weight also decreases.

(f) Describe what happens to the mass and weight of astronauts as they travel from the Earth to the Moon.

QUESTIONS

1 Uranus has a mass more than 14 times the Earth's. Venus has a mass which is slightly smaller than the Earth's. If you look at the information on these pages you will find that the gravitational field at the surface of Uranus is slightly smaller than the much smaller planet Venus, which has less mass. Why is this?

2 There is a point between the Earth and the Moon where the pull of the Earth is the same as the pull of the Moon. Explain why this would not be halfway between the two.

MODELS OF THE SOLAR SYSTEM

TOPIC CHECKLIST

- What did people believe in the past?
- What is the model we use today?
- What orbits what?

What did people believe in the past?

Early civilisations on the Earth studied the movement of the Sun and stars and saw that they seemed to move across the sky. They were able to predict with quite incredible accuracy what the movements would be for hundreds of years into the future. As science became more advanced, people tried to work out why the stars, Moon and Sun moved as they did. People believed that the Earth was the centre of the universe. When they tried to explain the movement of the Sun, planets and stars with the Earth at the centre of the solar system, they had to invent very complicated explanations.

Model of universe with Earth at centre

ⓐ Why is it possible to make very accurate predictions about the movement of the Moon, Sun and stars?

Copernicus (1473–1543) believed that the Sun was at the centre of the solar system with the planets **orbiting** (moving) round it. Galileo was an important scientist and publicly said that he preferred Copernicus' model of the solar system to the one accepted by scientists generally. This made Galileo very unpopular with the Roman Catholic Church and lead to him being sentenced to life imprisonment for his views. It was not until 1992, several hundred years later, that the Vatican acknowledged the Church was in error.

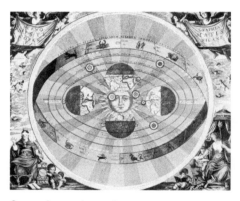

Copernican solar system

ⓑ Galileo is also famous for developing the telescope. Why would this have helped him with his theories about the movement of the planets?

Early in the 17th century Johannes Kepler developed Galileo's model further. He did calculations from data other scientists had collected and worked out that the planets had orbits that were **elliptical** (not quite round) in shape.

What is the model we use today?

Sir Isaac Newton used his own ideas about gravity and Kepler's work on elliptical orbits, and created a

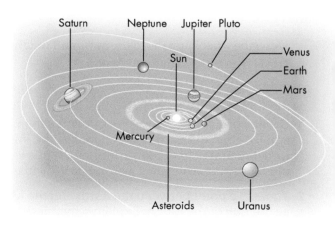

Present day elliptical model of solar system

mathematical model. He used the masses of objects and their distances apart to describe the movements of masses in the solar system with the Sun at the centre. Our present day model of the solar system has not changed much since Newton's time although it has been extended, for example, by the discovery of more planets.

What orbits what?

At the centre of our model of the solar system is the star we call the Sun. The Sun is an enormous ball of very hot gas. Compared to the Earth it has 330 000 times more mass and is over 100 times the diameter of the Earth.

The enormous mass of the Sun pulls the planets towards it, and because they are moving quickly, the gravitational force of the Sun keeps them moving in orbits around the Sun.

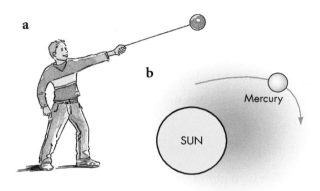

c Look at the diagram. What pulls the planets towards the Sun?

a When somebody swings a mass in a circle, the string pulls the mass towards the hand; b Mercury moves roughly on a circle around the Sun. Gravity pulls Mercury towards the Sun and keeps Mercury in orbit

As well as planets, other natural objects orbiting the Sun are asteroids, which are fairly small lumps of rock mostly in an orbit between Mars and Jupiter.

d What is the difference between asteroids and planets?

The Earth has a Moon which orbits the Earth just as the Earth orbits the Sun. The Earth has one moon, but Jupiter, Saturn, Neptune and Uranus have several moons orbiting them. Moons are held in place, like planets, by the gravitational force between the two masses.

e At least one asteroid has its own 'moon' which is another smaller asteroid. What do you think keeps the small asteroid orbiting the larger one?

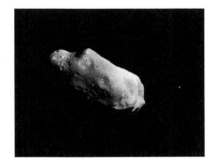

Asteroid 243 Ida and its moon

QUESTIONS

1 What reasons do you think ancient civilisations had for studying the stars?

2 Why does the time taken for different Moons of Jupiter to orbit the planet range from a few hours to several years?

3 Some planets take a long time to orbit the Sun. Why did Johannes Kepler rely on the data that other people had collected rather than just make his own measurements of the movement of the planets?

4 Ganymede, one of the moons of Jupiter, is in fact bigger than the planets Mercury and Pluto. Why is Ganymede a moon and not a planet?

5 The asteroid Ceres has a diameter of 932 km. The Moon, Miranda, which orbits Uranus has a diameter of 470 km, about half the size of Ceres. Why is Ceres not called a moon?

SATELLITES

What are satellites?

A **satellite** is an object that orbits a larger mass. The Earth is a satellite of the Sun, and the Moon is a satellite of the Earth. These are **natural satellites**. **Artificial satellites** are ones that humans have put into orbit. To get a satellite into orbit a lot of energy is required to overcome the Earth's gravity, as with rockets going to the Moon. The higher the orbit above the Earth, the more energy is required to get it there.

What kinds of orbit do we use?

At 36 000 km above the Earth's Equator there are a number of satellites. At this height, the time that the satellite takes to orbit the Earth is exactly 1 day. This means that the satellite stays exactly above one point on the Earth. This 'non-moving' effect is called **geostationary**. This allows people on the Earth to send and receive signals to and from a satellite 24 hours a day without having to worry about where the satellite might be in relation to the Earth and sending the signal in the right direction. Once a satellite dish is correctly aligned, the dish never needs to be moved.

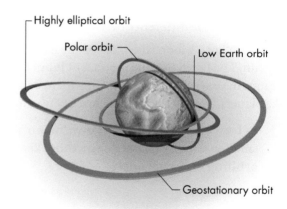

Types of orbit

Other satellites orbit at lower heights and complete several orbits in a day. There are also other types of orbit.

- Polar orbiting satellites pass over the poles of the Earth
- Low Earth orbit satellites have very short orbit times
- Highly elliptical orbit satellites move further from and closer to the Earth each time they make an orbit.

What is the history of satellites?

When the first satellite was launched in 1957 it made news headlines around the world: nowadays they are just part of life. Since then hundreds of satellites have been launched and many of these have since fallen back to Earth, usually burning up in the Earth's atmosphere.

These are some of the key milestones in satellite technology:

Name	Launch date	Function
Sputnik 1	4th October 1957	None
Explorer 1	1st February 1958	Found hints of radiation belt
US Tiros 1	1st April 1960	First weather satellite
Early Bird	6th April 1965	First commercial, geostationary communications satellite
GPS satellites	Complete system March 1994	Allow accurate location anywhere on the Earth's surface

(a) Sputnik 1 didn't send any signals. What was the point of launching it?

(b) What advantages do Low Earth orbit satellites have for photographing the Earth's surface?

(c) Why do people who live near the North pole have trouble receiving signals from geostationary satellites?

Why launch satellites?

Geostationary satellites are used for studying the weather, navigation and communications. Many people use signals from satellites to receive television pictures and make telephone calls around the world using geostationary satellites.

Polar satellites are used mainly to study weather and provide navigation signals. These satellites are no good for communication as they keep going out of sight if you are on the ground.

Satellites in highly elliptical orbits are used for communications for people who live close to the North Pole, as it is difficult for them to receive signals from the geostationary satellites above the equator.

Low Earth orbit satellites are used mainly for reconnaissance, as they pass over the Earth's surface only a few hundred kilometres up and can be used to photograph the surface of the Earth in great detail.

How do satellites tell us where we are?

The GPS (global positioning system) uses 24 satellites orbiting the Earth in six sets of orbits. At any moment, a receiver on the ground can receive the signals from at least four satellites. With the information the satellites send, the receiver works out exactly where it is to within a few metres. Cars use this system to tell drivers not only where they are, but also the best route to take.

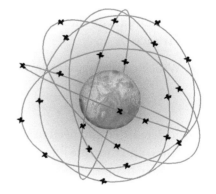

QUESTIONS

1 Explain what geostationary means.

2 The Moon is a satellite of the Earth. What is the Earth a satellite of?

3 Why is great care taken to make sure all the parts of a satellite work reliably before it is launched?

4 Why do you think that many satellites are solar powered?

K Speeding up

K1 HOW FAST IS IT MOVING?

TOPIC CHECKLIST

- Why do we measure speed?
- How is speed calculated?
- How can we measure speed?
- What is average speed?

Why do we measure speed?

Car drivers need to know how fast they are moving to make sure they are not exceeding the speed limit. The speedometer in front of the driver gives a measure of speed.

Sometimes we are more interested in the time taken to go a certain distance. Athletes need to know the time they take to run a race so they can tell if they have broken the records set by others. The 100 metres sprint race takes about ten seconds at the top competition level. The faster someone runs, the shorter the time they take to finish the race.

(a) **Use the data on the right to work out which runner won the race.**

(b) **Which runner had the lowest speed?**

How is speed calculated?

To calculate speed you need to know the **distance** something has moved and the **time** it took to move. The distance can be measured in many different units such as mm, cm, m, km, or miles. Time can be measured in seconds, minutes, or hours. Some of the units for speed which you will be familiar with are miles per hour for cars and metres per second for the speed of sound.

(c) **How many metres is (i) 300 cm (ii) 47 cm (iii) 2 km (iv) 0.15 km?**

(d) **How many seconds is (i) 2 minutes (ii) half an hour (iii) 300 ms?**

Times from an international 100 m race	
Lane	Time in seconds
1	10.45
2	11.51
3	11.34
4	10.40
5	10.55
6	10.26
7	11.04
8	11.11

To calculate speed we use this equation:

$$\text{speed (in metres per second)} = \frac{\text{distance (in metres)}}{\text{time (in seconds)}}$$

Scientists usually use the SI units of metres per second for speed as shown by the equation above.

e **If a rabbit runs 50 metres in 10 seconds, how fast is it running?**

The three calculations below are all of objects moving at the same speed. Notice how the answers look different depending on the units being used.

If a car moves 90 miles in 2 hours $\text{speed} = \dfrac{\text{distance}}{\text{time}}$ $\text{speed} = \dfrac{90 \text{ miles}}{2 \text{ hours}}$ $\text{speed} = 45$ miles per hour	If a bus travels 108 kilometres in 1½ hours $\text{speed} = \dfrac{\text{distance}}{\text{time}}$ $\text{speed} = \dfrac{108 \text{ kilometres}}{1.5 \text{ hours}}$ $\text{speed} = 72$ kilometres per hour	If a cheetah runs 60 metres in 3 seconds $\text{speed} = \dfrac{\text{distance}}{\text{time}}$ $\text{speed} = \dfrac{60 \text{ metres}}{3 \text{ seconds}}$ $\text{speed} = 20$ metres per second

How can we measure speed?

One of the most common techniques for measuring speed in science experiments is to use a light gate. A piece of card 10 cm wide is stuck to a trolley. When the trolley moves past the light gate, the front end of the card breaks the light beam and starts the timer. When the back end of the card moves away from the light beam the timer stops. You can use the time measured and the distance from the front to the back of the card to calculate the speed of the trolley.

Light gate experiment

The calculation on the right is the result of Jackie's experiment. Notice that Jackie changed the distance measurement from cm to m so that she could calculate the speed in metres per second.

f **Another experiment using the same equipment, showed the same card on the trolley breaking the light beam for 0.1 seconds. Calculate the speed the trolley was moving at.**

Card width = 0.1 metres (10 cm) Time light beam broken = 0.2 seconds $\text{speed} = \dfrac{\text{distance}}{\text{time}}$ $\text{speed} = \dfrac{0.1 \text{ metres}}{0.2 \text{ seconds}}$ $\text{speed} = 0.5$ metres per second

What is average speed?

When an athlete runs a 100 metres sprint, they are moving faster at the end of the race than at the beginning. The speed calculated is an average speed for the whole race. It averages out when the athlete is running slower or faster. In this case athletes start at 0 m/s and when they finish the race they may be moving at over 15 m/s. If the race took 10 seconds, the average speed would be 10 m/s. The average speed does not tell us the speed of the athlete at any particular point in the race.

QUESTIONS

1 If a bird flies 200 metres in 1 minute and 40 seconds, what is its speed?

2 A river flows from the mountains to the sea. The length of the river is 144 kilometres and it takes 3 days for water to get from the source of the river to the sea. What is the average speed of the river in kilometres per hour?

3 In question 2 you calculated the average speed. How do you think the speed of the river varies along its length?

Speeding up

103

Faster and faster

Sometimes the speed of an object changes. For example, it may start moving faster and faster.

When James starts from the top of a hill on his bicycle and moves down the hill without pedalling, he moves faster and faster. At the start when he first lets the brakes off, he is not moving so his speed is 0 m/s. As he starts to move down the hill his speed is low. Gradually he speeds up. His speed is changing all the time because he is speeding up all the time. The scientific word for speeding up is **accelerating**.

Distance travelled in metres	Time taken in seconds
0	0
3	5
10	10
23	15
40	20
63	25

Distance and time for James freewheeling down a hill

a From the table work out James' average speed from the top of the hill to the bottom.

b The table gives the distance moved in each 5 second interval. Calculate the average speeds for each 5 second interval.

c Describe how the speed of the cyclist changes.

We can get similar data by doing an experiment in the laboratory with a slope and a trolley. The photograph on the right shows the set up of the equipment. The trolley starts from a speed of 0 m/s. The time taken to pass through each light gate is measured, as well as the time to get from one light gate to another.

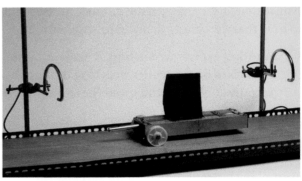

Light gate experiment for acceleration

The measurements and calculations from an experiment using two light gates are shown.

Light gate 1 at 1 m Beam broken for 0.22 seconds speed = $\dfrac{\text{distance}}{\text{time}}$ speed = $\dfrac{0.1 \text{ metres}}{0.22 \text{ seconds}}$ speed = 0.45 metres per second **Speed at first light gate = 0.45 m/s**	*Light gate 2 at 2 m* Beam broken for 0.16 seconds speed = $\dfrac{\text{distance}}{\text{time}}$ speed = $\dfrac{0.1 \text{ metres}}{0.16 \text{ seconds}}$ speed = 0.63 metres per second **Speed at second light gate = 0.63 m/s**	*Other information:* Time for trolley to move down slope = 6.3 seconds Length of slope = 2 metres speed = $\dfrac{\text{distance}}{\text{time}}$ speed = $\dfrac{2 \text{ metres}}{6.3 \text{ seconds}}$ speed = 0.32 m/s Average speed of trolley = 0.32 m/s

The average speed is calculated using the total distance from the top to the bottom of the ramp and the total time taken. The time to pass each light gate tells us the speed of the trolley at each light gate. As you can see it is moving faster at the second light gate. The trolley is speeding up all the time.

What happens when the slope is steeper?

When riding his bike downhill, James notices that he speeds up more when moving down steeper slopes.

d Describe an experiment you could do in the laboratory to investigate this effect.

What happens when the object has more mass?

One day, James is having a freewheeling race (no pedalling) down a hill with his friends. James' friend Sonata is lighter than James and feels that she will not speed up as much as James down the hill, but she finishes just in front. In fact, the mass of an object does not affect how it speeds up under the pull of gravity. The next time she raced James, Sonata found that if she bent down low over the handlebars to reduce air resistance, she finished well in front. Friction and wind resistance do affect how much things speed up.

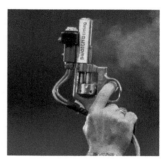

Using electronic timing

e How could you investigate in the laboratory whether mass affects how objects speed up?

Measuring time accurately

Most schools have a sports day: track events like sprint races or 1500 metres are timed using stop watches. The finish-line judges sit in line with the finish line and start their stop-watches when they see the smoke from the starter's gun. They stop the watches when the runners cross the finish line. This method is accurate enough for school athletic events as it gives times accurate to about 0.5 seconds.

In international athletics races the time must be measured much more accurately because the performances of the top athletes are often within a few hundredths of a second of each other. Human timers are not accurate enough to do this because their reaction time is too slow, so electronic equipment is used. The electronic timers are connected to the starter's gun and start automatically when it is fired. The timer records the time when each runner breaks a light beam across the track. The accuracy of the timing devices we use depends on what is being measured and for what purpose.

QUESTIONS

1 Why do time judges use the smoke from the gun rather than the sound from it?

2 Why are times at a school event not usually measured to the nearest hundredth of a second?

3 You have a choice of a tape measure marked in cm and a metre rule marked in mm.

  a Which would you use if you were making furniture? Why?

  b Which would you use if you were measuring the distance of a shot put throw? Why?

4 Describe how the slope of a ramp and mass of an object can affect how the object speeds up.

TOPIC CHECKLIST

- How can things travel at a steady speed?
- What happens when forces are balanced?
- How do unbalanced forces affect movement?
- How does mass affect speeding up?

Ice skater

How can things travel at a steady speed?

We are used to things around us slowing down unless we keep pushing them. If you stop pedalling on a bicycle on a flat road, the friction of the tyres and air resistance are forces which will slow you down. If we were able to start something moving and then remove all the forces on it, it would carry on moving at a constant speed in a straight line forever. Obviously, this would be unusual in everyday life as friction affects most things. Ice-skating is one situation where there is very little friction and so the skater only slows down very gradually.

Air track

If we want to investigate speed with almost no friction we can do so using an air track. Air is pushed up through holes in the surface and allows the vehicle above to move on a cushion of air without touching the track. We can use light gates again to find out what is happening to the speed of the vehicle as it moves along the track.

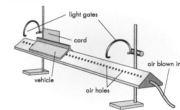

This vehicle is going at constant speed

ⓐ **What would you expect to notice about the time measured by the light gate at each end of the track?**

What happens when forces are balanced?

In the air track experiment, the force of friction on the vehicle is almost zero, so the vehicle continues to move at a constant speed. In fact, it would slow down very gradually because of air resistance.

The forces are balanced when the trolley moves at constant speed

When you stop pushing a supermarket trolley, friction slows it down. You can keep it moving at a constant speed by applying a steady push. This push balances the friction forces that would make it slow down and keeps it going at a constant speed. The forces are balanced.

If the same trolley is standing still, it remains stationary if the forces on it are balanced. It will stay still if two children try to push it in opposite directions. The forces are balanced.

ⓑ **Describe the forces acting on a car travelling at a constant speed on the motorway.**

When the forces are balanced, the trolley stays stationary

How do unbalanced forces affect movement?

The experiment shown below is used to investigate the effect of different forces on a trolley. Pupils doing the experiment found that as the force pulling the trolley gets bigger, the trolley speeds up more. They correctly came up with the statement "The bigger the force, the more the object will speed up."

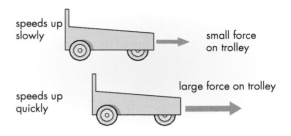

Unbalanced forces can also change the direction of movement. If Jane was pushing a supermarket trolley along and then Mark came along and started to push the trolley from the side, it would change direction without slowing down.

How does mass affect speeding up?

How much an object speeds up depends on the size of the force on it and the mass of the object. If the same force is acting on two objects of different mass, the one with the bigger mass will speed up less than the one with the smaller mass.

This shopping trolley has high mass

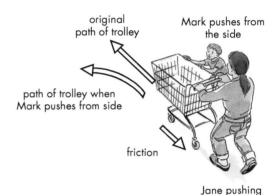

This trolley changes direction

c **What happens when there are unbalanced forces on an object which is not moving?**

Moving away at traffic lights, the empty lorry gets faster, quicker

d **What is the effect on the speeding up of the lorry if it has no load?**

One of the reasons that a heavy lorry needs a more powerful engine than a car is that it takes more force to speed up the heavy load that the lorry carries.

QUESTIONS

1 When a space craft is moving in space at a constant speed, it does not need to have its engines running, but an aircraft flying through air does. Explain why there is this difference.

2 Heavy lorries have more powerful engines than sports cars, but they speed up less, why is this?

3 If there is no friction between the vehicle on an air track and the track, why does the vehicle eventually slow down and stop?

HOW CAN WE INCREASE SPEED?

How does shape help?

A racing cyclist has very little friction when moving slowly. Racing bikes have very narrow and hard tyres to reduce friction with the road as much as possible. When a racing cyclist starts to move quickly, the amount of air resistance increases dramatically.

To reduce the air resistance which works against cyclists they lower their bodies to try to give themselves a shape which moves through the air easily. Experience shows us that for most situations the best shape is rounded at the front and pointed at the back. We call this a **streamlined** shape.

Streamlined shapes

Nature has produced excellent streamlined shapes; perhaps the best examples are fish and dolphins. Their ability to move quickly through the water and overcome water resistance is important. This may be either to get away from predators or to catch other fish. Submarines use this same streamlined shape.

Some of the fastest cars ever built are very similar in shape to a fish, to reduce the friction slowing them down.

a **Although modern cars are fairly streamlined, why do they not have long narrow tails?**

How does speed affect air resistance?

Even the most streamlined objects still have some air resistance and the force of air resistance increases with speed. So the only way to speed something up is either to further cut air resistance or to increase the thrust or force pushing it forwards.

A car moving at a steady 60 km/h over 100 km consumes less fuel than if it moved at 80 km/h for 100 km, even though it travels the same distance. The table on the right shows the fuel consumption of a car.

Fuel consumption figures, family saloon	
60 km/h	6 litres per 100 km
80 km/h	7.5 litres per 100 km

At higher speeds much more thrust is needed from the engine to push the car forwards against the increased air resistance. Although the car takes a shorter time to cover the same distance than a slower car, it needs more fuel overall because of the extra thrust needed to overcome air resistance.

ⓑ How much less fuel will a car travelling 100 km use if it moves at 60 km/h rather than 80 km/h?

How does friction make things hot?

In some situations, the friction force from the air on a moving object becomes very large. When a space capsule re-enters Earth's atmosphere, it is moving very fast indeed. The friction between the air and the surface of the space ship causes the surface to become red hot.

The movement of any object through air makes the air particles move about more. They have more kinetic energy, so the temperature of the air is increased. In the case of re-entry of a spacecraft, the amount of energy given to the air particles is enormous so the air becomes very hot. The surface of the spacecraft also becomes very hot because it is being hit by air particles at many thousands of kilometres per hour. The particles in the surface of the spacecraft will vibrate a great deal. The result is that a lot of heat is generated.

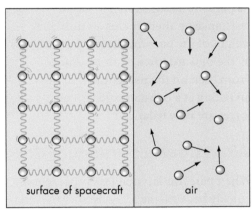

surface of spacecraft   air

Vibrating particles generate heat

ⓒ Rubbing your hands together makes them feel hot. Use the particle theory to explain why this is.

QUESTIONS

1 Use the particle theory to explain why a streamlined shape moves through air or water more quickly.

2 Describe three situations where streamlined shapes are used. Don't use the ones on these pages.

3 Some fish are definitely not streamlined, like the one shown on the right; why do you think this is?

4 Aluminium has a low density and a low melting point. In what ways would these properties be good and bad for a space shuttle?

HOW DO PARACHUTES WORK?

TOPIC CHECKLIST

- What is freefall parachuting?
- What does a parachute do?
- Distance–time graphs
- Speed–time graphs

What is freefall parachuting?

When parachutists first jump from a plane, they fall freely getting faster and faster because the force of gravity pulling them down is bigger than the force of air resistance pushing up. The force is unbalanced.

As parachutists gain speed, the air resistance on them increases until the weight of the parachutist is balanced by the upward force of air resistance. From then on the parachutist carries on falling at a constant speed. The forces are now balanced.

small air resistance

parachutist speeds up

weight larger than air resistance

What does a parachute do?

When parachutists open their parachutes, they slow down very quickly because the air resistance to the large parachute is much larger than the weight of the parachutist. The parachutist slows down until the air resistance is once again balanced by the weight of the parachutist. The fall continues at a slower constant speed.

a **Explain the effect on the fall of the parachutist if he or she used a larger parachute.**

air resistance

weight

When the parachute is open the forces are balanced.

Distance–time graphs

We can draw a graph showing the distance things move and the time they take. This is called a **distance–time graph**. On the right there is a distance–time graph for a coach journey. We can see from the graph that there are times when the slope of the graph is quite steep: the steeper the slope the faster the coach was moving. When the graph line is horizontal, the coach had stopped.

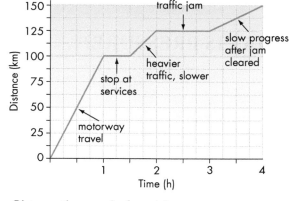

Distance–time graph of coach journey

b What is the average speed of the coach in the first hour?

c What is the average speed of the coach for the whole of the journey shown on the graph?

d Explain why the answer to the second question above is less than the answer to the first one.

Speed–time graphs

Another type of graph shows how speed changes with time. On this graph an upward slope to the line shows the car getting faster and a horizontal line shows constant speed.

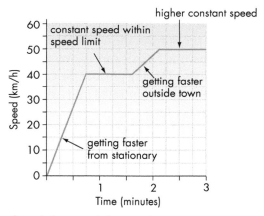

Speed–time graph for a car journey

QUESTIONS

1 Parachutes do not stop us falling, they just make us fall more slowly. Use the idea of balanced forces to explain this.

2 What factors affect the speed a parachutist falls, when the parachute is open? Explain the effect of each factor.

3 A feather and a ruler have roughly the same size and shape. Explain why they fall differently on the earth.

4 A piece of paper crumpled into a ball falls more quickly than the same piece of paper if it is left flat. Explain why this is.

L Pressure and moments

L1 WHAT IS PRESSURE?

> **TOPIC CHECKLIST**
>
> ● Pressure, force and area
> ● How do we calculate pressure?
> ● What is the pressure under our feet?
> ● What are pascals?

Pressure, force and area

You have studied how forces can change the shape of objects and make objects move. If a force pushes on a solid that cannot be squashed, like concrete, the effect is called **pressure**.

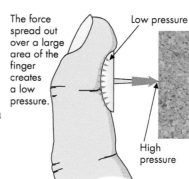

The force spread out over a large area of the finger creates a low pressure.

Low pressure

The force concentrated into a small area at the point of the pin creates high pressure.

High pressure

The drawing pin shown on the right is being pushed into a cork-board. The pressure on the head of the drawing pin and the finger is low because the force is spread over a large area. The pressure on the point of the drawing pin and the cork-board is high because the same force is concentrated into a small area. When we use the same amount of force:

● the force on a small area gives high pressure

● the force on a large area gives low pressure

The effect of pressure can be seen in many everyday situations. Camels have evolved wide feet to spread the weight of the camel so that the pressure on the sand is lower. This allows them to walk on sand without sinking in.

Camels have big feet

People use the same idea when walking on snow with snow shoes. A person who is heavier will exert more pressure on the snow than a lighter person even if they are wearing snow shoes with the same area.

On the same area:

● a small force gives low pressure

● a large force gives high pressure

(a) **What two things could a furniture maker do to reduce the pressure of the feet of a cupboard on carpets?**

(b) **If you sat on one nail it would be painful, yet some people are able to lie on a bed of nails without being injured. How is this possible?**

Snow shoes are used because people have small feet

How do we calculate pressure?

To calculate pressure we need to measure the size of the force applied and the size of the area to which the force is applied. Area is usually measured in square metres (m^2). Force is measured in newtons (N).

To calculate pressure, divide the force by the area.

$$\text{pressure} = \frac{\text{force in N}}{\text{area in } m^2}$$

Pressure is measured in units called newtons per square metre or N/m^2.

L

> The pressure under an elephant's feet can be calculated.
>
> Each foot has an area of about $0.2\ m^2$
>
> It has four feet on the ground, so the total area is around $0.8\ m^2$
>
> The elephant weighs 50 000 newtons, so this is the force.
>
> $$\text{pressure} = \frac{\text{force}}{\text{area}}$$
>
> $$\text{pressure} = \frac{50\ 000\ N}{0.8\ m^2} = 62\ 500\ N/m^2$$
>
> The pressure under an elephant's foot is around **62 500 N/m^2**

What is the pressure under our feet?

When we stand, all of our weight acts downwards through our feet. To calculate the pressure under our feet we need to know the force and the area the force acts on.

Jo weighs 500 N and is wearing stiletto heels which together have an area of 1 cm^2 (0.0001 m^2). She exerts a pressure of about 5 000 000 N/m^2.

c Calculate the pressure that a man weighing 800 N will produce under his feet if together they have an area of 0.05 m^2.

What are pascals?

The French philosopher, mathematician, and physicist, Blaise Pascal, gave his name to the SI unit of pressure, the pascal (Pa). 1 Pa is equivalent to 1 N/m^2. The pressure under Jo's bare feet would be:

$$\text{pressure} = \frac{\text{force}}{\text{area}}$$

$$\text{pressure} = \frac{500N}{0.02\ m^2}$$

$$\text{pressure} = 25\ 000\ N/m^2 \text{ or } 25\ 000\ Pa \text{ or } 25\ kPa$$

d Explain why the pressure changes when Jo takes off her shoes and stands barefoot.

QUESTIONS

1 Use the idea of pressure to explain why a sharp knife cuts better than a blunt one.

2 Skis are flat on the bottom so that they do not sink into soft snow. When a skier turns they use the sharp edge of the ski to dig into hard snow. Explain how these two uses of the skis work.

3 Look back at the calculation of pressure for an elephant and for Jo. Would it hurt more to be trodden on by the elephant or Jo? Explain your answer.

4 A box stands on the floor. It has a weight of 250 newtons. The area of the box that rests on the floor is 0.25 m^2. Calculate the pressure under the box.

WHAT IS HYDRAULICS?

Hydraulics

If you put some water in a balloon and squeeze it, the liquid in the balloon will change shape as a result of the pressure you apply to it with your hands. Liquids generally cannot be forced into a smaller space or volume.

If you put your finger over the end of a syringe full of water, you will find it impossible to push the plunger in, because the particles in liquids are quite close together and they cannot be pushed any closer together.

In the experiment below, pushing the first plunger produces pressure in the liquid which is the same throughout the liquid. The pressure acts equally in all directions. The push is transmitted through the liquid from the first plunger to the second plunger, which moves out.

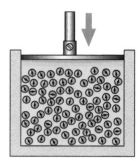

As there is little or no space between the particles in a liquid, it cannot be compressed

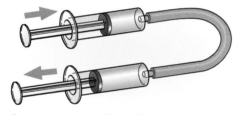

Pressure acts equally in all directions

The diagram on the right shows a syringe with holes drilled in it. Because the pressure is equal in all directions in a liquid, the water squirts equally in all directions.

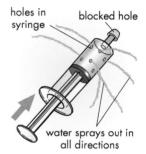

water sprays out in all directions

Hydraulic systems

The hydraulic system below shows two syringes of different sizes, joined together. If the small syringe's plunger is pushed with a force of 2 newtons, the large plunger will be pushed out with a force of 10 newtons. The reasons for this increase in force, **amplification**, are shown in the calculation.

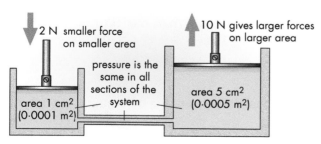

Pushing one syringe plunger in makes the other move out

Force on small plunger = 2 N

Area of small plunger = 0.0001 m²

pressure in small syringe $= \dfrac{\text{force}}{\text{area}}$

pressure in small syringe $= \dfrac{2}{0.0001} = 20\,000$ N/m²

The pressure in the large syringe will be the same.

the force in the large syringe = pressure × area

force = 20 000 × 0.0005 = 10 N

So the force on the large syringe plunger is 10 N, which shows the 2 N force on the small plunger has been amplified.

However, you don't get something for nothing. Although the force increases, the distance the second piston moves is five times less than the distance you move the first piston.

Hydraulics are used in car braking systems. A small piston is pressed with a small force at one end of a tube by pressing on the brake pedal, and a larger piston is pushed out at the other end with a much larger force.

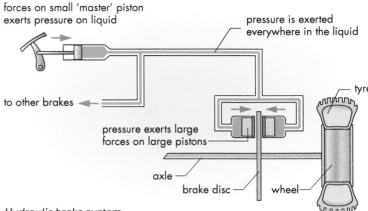

Hydraulic brake system

(a) **What benefit is there to the driver of a car, using a hydraulic brake system like the one shown here?**

(b) **Why do you think the walls of the pipes that carry hydraulic fluid are very thick?**

Water pressure

Water has weight because the gravity of the Earth pulls it down towards the centre of the Earth. So like any other object it can also exert a pressure. We call this water pressure.

If you were to swim down 10 metres underwater, the pressure from the water above you would be much more than if you were only 1 metre below the surface of the water.

It is important to realise that it is not the *volume* of water above you that causes the pressure but the *depth* of water above you.

(c) **Why are divers' watches pressurised?**

In parts of the countryside that are flat, water towers are frequently used to create a **head** of water. The weight of water at the top of the tower pushes down on water below and pressurises it.

QUESTIONS

1 Look at the drawing of a hydraulic rod cutter on the right. Explain how it works.

2 Why must the handle move a lot further than the cutting piston?

3 Above the hot water tank in a house, there is a large water container. Why is it always higher up than the hot water tank?

4 Dams are always built with thicker walls at the bottom than at the top. Why do you think this is?

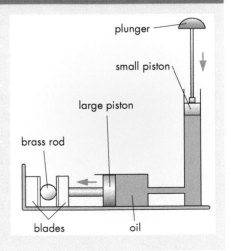

System for cutting brass rods

WHAT IS PNEUMATICS?

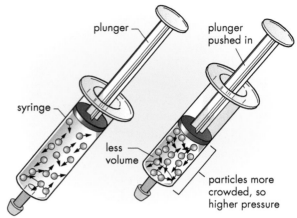

Gas being compressed

Pneumatics

Pneumatics is to do with how gases behave under pressure. The start of the word pneumatic 'pneu' is also found in other words that are related to air and pressure, pneumatic tyres, pneumonia.

If you block the end of an air-filled syringe with your finger, it is quite easy to push the plunger in. The particles in a gas are not very close together so it is possible to squeeze them closer together so they take up less space or volume. This is called **compressing** a gas. It puts the gas under pressure.

What causes gas pressure in a container?

Gas pressure can be explained using the particle theory. The particles in a container are moving around quickly. Some of them are colliding with the inside of the container and as they bounce off, they push the container away. As this force acts over an area, there is a pressure on the container, caused by the gas. Particles colliding in the middle of the gas cause pressure inside the gas too.

If a container is made smaller, for example, the plunger of a syringe is pushed in, the space the particles move around in gets smaller too. This means more collisions will happen on each square centimetre of the surface of the syringe, which means the pressure increases.

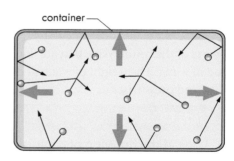

Gas pressure

Another way of increasing the pressure is to put more particles into a container. This is what happens when you pump up a tyre. More particles mean more collisions and so the pressure increases.

  ⓐ **Explain why the pressure in a car tyre goes down if you let some air out.**

  ⓑ **Use the particle theory to explain why the pressure inside a bicycle pump increases when you push the plunger in as you pump.**

How do aerosols work?

The aerosol on the right has a gas space above the liquid. This gas is under pressure and when the valve is opened by pressing the button, the high pressure gas inside the container can expand into the space outside the can where the pressure is lower. The expanding gas forces the liquid out of the nozzle.

If the aerosol is thrown onto a fire, the gas inside gets hot. This makes the particles speed up and bump into the sides of the container harder. If the gas gets hot enough, the pressure caused by the fast particles bouncing around can be enough to make the container explode.

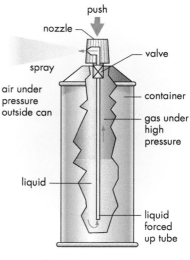

Cross-section of aerosol can

C **Explain why the aerosol is not completely filled with liquid.**

Gas pressure

Gas pressure is one of the most important ways of making machines move. An example is the steam engine, which uses the gas pressure from water turning into steam inside a small space in a cylinder. Steam takes up more space so the pressure in the cylinder increases and pushes the piston out. The movement of the piston turns a wheel. The effect is a bit like the opposite of pushing in the plunger in a syringe.

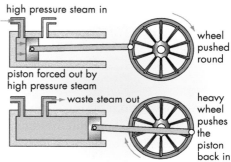

How a steam engine works

Atmospheric pressure

The gas does not have to be inside a container to exert a pressure, the air all around us is made up of particles that are bombarding us all the time. As they bounce off us they are squashing us, this is called **atmospheric pressure**.

On the Earth's surface, we are at the bottom of a 'sea' of air. Gravity is pulling the air downwards, and the deeper we are in the air, the more weight of air there is above us squashing us. This means that when people climb hills the pressure around them is lower than for people at sea level.

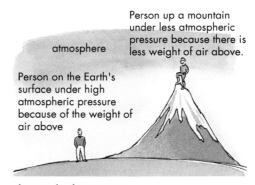

Atmospheric pressure

QUESTIONS

1 Describe the effect on the particles in a gas when the gas is heated and how this increases the pressure of the gas in a container.

2 Why do you think air is used in tyres rather than water?

3 Air becomes 'thinner' as you climb a mountain because the particles are further apart. Use the particle theory to explain why this results in lower pressure.

4 Mechanics always make sure there is no air in a hydraulic brake system. Why do you think this is so important?

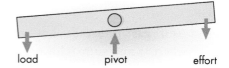

load   pivot   effort

Parts of a lever

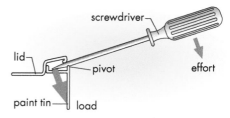

screwdriver

lid   pivot   effort

paint tin   load

Long levers, less effort: opening a can of paint with a screw driver

Levers

A lever is a simple machine which uses a **pivot**. A pivot is the point around which something turns. We use many levers in everyday life. A door handle is a lever. Using a screwdriver to open a can of paint is a lever. A lever turns around a pivot. The force we apply to the lever is called the **effort**. The force the lever pushes with is called the **load**.

How do levers amplify forces?

The further away from the pivot you apply a force the easier it is to turn the lever. If you shut the door by pushing close to the hinge, you have to use quite a lot of effort. When you push the door shut at the handle, the width of the door acts as a long lever to help you so you need less effort.

(a) **Why are door handles usually on the opposite edge of the door from the hinge?**

It is easier to push the door open or closed if you push a long way from the hinge

To tighten a nut on a bicycle, you push at the end of the spanner furthest away from the nut. For larger nuts where the forces are greater, we use longer spanners.

Levers in our bodies

When we move around and walk we use a system of levers in our bodies. Even eating relies on the lever formed by our jaw.

If we look carefully at human teeth, we can again see the effect of distance from the pivot coming into play.

- The teeth that are furthest away from the pivot of the jaw are used to cut with sharp edges. These do not need a lot of force to do their job.

- The teeth that need more force are positioned close to the pivot, and so the muscles closing the jaw create a greater force here.

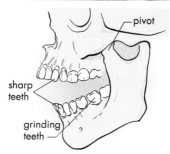

pivot

sharp teeth

grinding teeth

Our arms are levers, the elbow is the pivot and the bone is the lever. To make our arms move we use muscles, but muscles only apply a force in one direction, so to make our arm move up and down, we need two muscles. We use the biceps muscle to bend the arm and the triceps muscle to straighten the arm.

These two muscles are called **antagonistic muscles** as they work against each other. When you bend your arm the triceps relax and the biceps contract. When you straighten your arm the triceps contract and the biceps relax. The biceps are larger than the triceps because we usually bend our arms to lift weights.

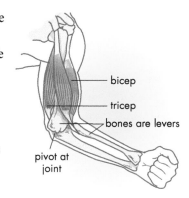

Arm muscles bending the arm at the elbow

Turning effects

We have seen that when a force is applied to one end of a lever it tries to turn the lever. This is called the **turning effect** of the force. The turning effect depends not only on the size of the force applied to the lever, but also on the distance from the pivot to where along the lever the force is applied. This distance is measured **perpendicular** to the force applied.

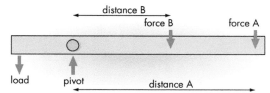

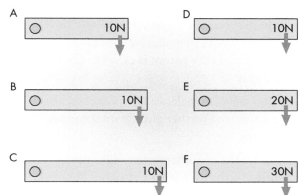

In the diagram on the right:

b Which of the forces A, B, C will have the greatest turning effect?

c Which of the forces D, E, F will have the greatest turning effect?

QUESTIONS

1 Copy the drawing of the nutcrackers and label the effort, load and pivot.

2 Use sketches to explain why the effort you use to lift a wheelbarrow is smaller then the load in the wheelbarrow

3 Explain why there are two antagonistic muscles used to control the movement of your leg at the knee.

4 Look at the photograph of the giant panda. Explain why the panda is using its back teeth to crush the bamboo shoots.

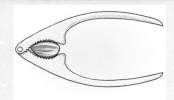

Nutcrackers

USING COUNTERWEIGHTS

How do things balance?

Seesaws help us understand balancing very well. A small child, Henry, is sitting on one end of the seesaw and his parent is sitting on the other. When they both pick up their feet, we know that the heavier parent will move downwards and Henry will be lifted into the air. The diagram shows this.

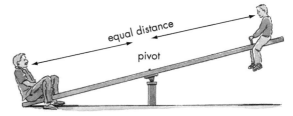

This seesaw is not balanced

We also know that to balance the seesaw, the parent needs to move closer to the pivot. What this means is that Henry, with a smaller weight, can balance the parent as long as the parent is closer to the pivot than Henry.

A smaller child can balance Henry, but the child would have to be further away from the pivot than Henry.

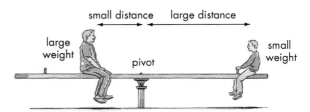

The seesaw is balanced when the parent is nearer to the pivot

You can see that the effect of a small force is magnified by the long lever to balance Henry. Alternatively, with a large force the lever can be shorter.

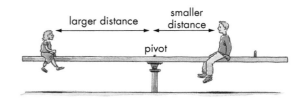

When a smaller child sits on one end, Henry has to move closer, to balance the seesaw

Balancing in life

There are many balancing problems in life. Kangaroos use their tails to balance themselves whilst travelling at speed or jumping. The pterodactyl had an extension to the back of its skull, which may have helped to balance its heavy beak.

Gymnasts frequently need to balance and they use one part of their body to balance another part. The photograph on the right shows an ice skater leaning forward and a leg held out behind to balance the weight of the body. This leg is being used as a **counterbalance**.

Cranes also use a counterbalance to make it possible to lift heavy loads without making the central support too thick. The counterbalance for this crane is on the left of the crane.

If any of these systems didn't have a counterbalance then they would topple over. The heavy part, such as the ice-skater's body, would make them fall over.

a Draw a diagram of the ice-skater and the crane. Label the load and the counterbalance.

b Explain why it is easier for one person to carry a ladder by holding it in the middle.

c Use a sketch to explain why people walking with a heavy rucksack lean forwards.

Lifting safely

When people lift heavy weights, they should do so without bending their backs. If you lift with a bent back, it produces very large forces in the spine and surrounding muscles.

QUESTIONS

1 Why are people who lift heavy loads advised to keep their backs vertical and bend their knees?

2 In car parks, the barrier usually has a counterbalance; how does this help?

3 Why do the people who load aircraft make sure that the weight in the hold is evenly spread?

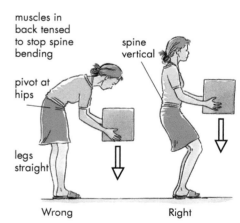

muscles in back tensed to stop spine bending

spine vertical

pivot at hips

legs straight

Wrong   Right

How to lift things safely

L6 MOMENTS

TOPIC CHECKLIST

- What is a moment?
- Balancing moments
- Unbalanced moments
- Testing the principle of moments

What is a moment?

The seesaw turns about a pivot. It is like a lever. The force each person puts on the end of the lever has a turning effect. The turning effect of a force on a lever is called the **moment**. The turning effect or the size of the moment, depends on the size of the force applied and on the distance between where the force is applied and the pivot.

The seesaw balancing can be explained more exactly by doing some calculations using the size of the force and the distance between the force and the pivot. This is called calculating the moment of a force.

We measure the force in newtons (N) and the distance in metres (m) so the units for moments are newton metres (Nm).

$400\,N \times 2\,m$ $200\,N \times 4\,m$
$= 800\,Nm$ $= 800\,Nm$

The two moments which make the seesaw balance are the same size.

Balancing moments

The force on the left is turning the left side anti-clockwise and the force on the right is turning the right side clockwise. When the anti-clockwise moment is equal to the clockwise moment then the two moments are balanced. This is called the **principle of moments**.

When something is balanced:

the sum of the anti-clockwise moments = the sum of the clockwise moments

Unbalanced moments

Often moments do not balance, but using the same methods of calculating moments can help us understand why they don't balance.

The seesaw on the right is not balanced. The calculations show why it isn't balanced.

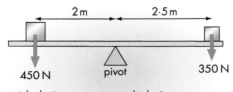

anticlockwise moment   clockwise moment
$450 \times 2 = 900\,Nm$ $350 \times 2.5 = 875\,Nm$

The seesaw will turn anticlockwise

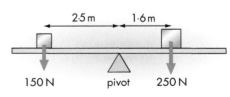

ⓐ **Calculate the moments for each of the forces in the diagram above and decide if the seesaw will balance.**

Testing the principle of moments

We can investigate the relationship between force and distance using a beam balance. The drawing on the right shows a situation where the balance is level, but the forces and distances are different on both sides.

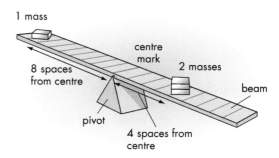

Beam balance used in laboratory

The table shows the results of an experiment using the set-up shown above. The number of masses and the number of spaces from the mass to the pivot are given for the left and right sides. The experiment shows five pairs of results A to E. You will notice that there are no units used in this experiment. We can calculate moments just the same by multiplying mass or weight (force) by space (distance).

Helen multiplied the force and distance on each side in the table to calculate the moment for each side.

ⓑ **Copy and complete the table shown on the right.**

ⓒ **Helen finds that the moments for one set of results did not balance, which one is this?**

Table of results for balance					
	A	B	C	D	E
Number of masses on left	1	3	2	2	3
Number of spaces on left	1	1	5	8	4
Number of masses on right	1	1	1	4	2
Number of spaces on right	1	3	1	4	6
Moment anti-clockwise	1	3	–	–	12
Moment clockwise	1	–	1	16	–

QUESTIONS

1 What force would need to be used in **A** to make it balance?

2 What distance from the pivot would the force in **B** need to be, to make it balance?

3 **C** does not balance. Where would you need to put a 25 N downward force to make it balance?

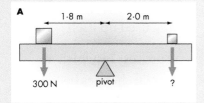

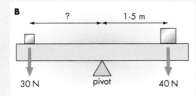

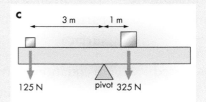

Glossary

accelerating getting faster

accumulate the build up of **pesticides** in animals towards the top of the food chain

acid rain rainwater that has reacted with acidic pollutants

adapted when plants, animals or cells have special features that help them to survive or do their job

addictive when a **drug** makes a person feel that they need it to get through the day

amplification force or movement made larger

antagonistic pair a pair of muscles that pull a bone in opposite directions

application rate the amount of **fertiliser** needed to fertilise 100 square metres of crop

asexual reproduction the type of reproduction which does not involve sex or sex cells

atmospheric pressure force on an area caused by air particles bouncing off a surface

balanced in equations, having the same kinds and numbers of atoms on each side of a **symbol equation**

balanced diet a diet that contains the correct balance of **nutrients** to stay healthy

bases the chemical opposites of acids

biological weathering rocks being weathered by the action of plants

biomass the mass of a living thing, usually measured dry (with water removed)

breathing system the organ system where air is taken into and out of the body, where oxygen enters the blood, and carbon dioxide is removed from the blood

burette a very accurate device for measuring liquids

carbonate a group of atoms: one carbon atom joined to three oxygen atoms

carnivores animals that eat only other animals

catalyst a substance that speeds up a chemical reaction without being used up itself

change of state the process by which a material changes between solid, liquid and gas

chemical energy a form of energy stored within chemicals

chemical reactions	the process of change from reactants to products	**deficiency**	what happens to a human or a plant when it does not get an adequate supply of a particular **nutrient**
chemical weathering	rocks being weathered by reacting with acidic rainwater	**digestive system**	the organ system where food is taken into the body, broken down, and absorbed into the blood
chlorophyll	the green substance within plant cells which helps to make food		
circulatory system	the organ system which pumps blood around the body	**diluted**	when a solution has had extra solvent added
clones	an identical copy of a living thing produced by **asexual reproduction**	**displacement**	a type of reaction where a metal is pushed out of its compound
compete	when two living things live in the same place and need the same resources	**dissipated**	spread out
		distance	length moved
		distance–time graph	graph that shows how **distance** moved changes with **time**
compressing	a squashing force		
concentrated	when a solution contains a lot of solute		
concentration	how **concentrated** a solution is	**drug**	a chemical that affects the way your body works
conservation of energy	law stating that the total amount of energy in a system does not change	**efficient**	acting with very little waste
		effort	force applied to do a task
		egg cell	the female sex cell in humans and plants
consumers	animals that must eat other living things for food		
counter-balance	a **mass** used to balance the **weight** of another mass	**electrolyte**	a liquid that conducts an electric current
		elliptical	oval-shaped

end point	during a **neutralisation** reaction, when the pH is exactly 7
energy conservation	where energy is used more efficiently
environmental variation	those features of a living thing which have been affected by its surroundings and lifestyle
fertilisation	when the nucleus of the male sex cell (**pollen cell** or **sperm cell**) and the nucleus of the female sex cell (**egg cell**) join together
fertilisers	chemicals that contain **nutrients** important for plants to grow and stay healthy
fitness	a measure of how well your heart and lungs deliver oxygen to the cells around your body
fitness programme	an organised programme which tells someone how much exercise to do, what to eat, and how to cut down on alcohol and cigarettes
Flue Gas Desulphur-ization plant	equipment to remove sulphur from smoke
food chains	a diagram showing what an animal eats and what eats it; a diagram showing the flow of energy through living things
food web	a diagram made of lots of joined up food chains, showing what eats what in a habitat; a diagram showing the flow of energy through all the living things in a habitat
fuel	a substance that burns to release energy
fuel cell	a device for changing chemical energy directly into electricity
generator	converts **kinetic energy** into electrical energy
genes	instructions inside the nucleus of each cell which contain information controlling a living thing's characteristics
geo-stationary	an orbit that keeps a satellite above one place on the Earth all the time
geo-stationary satellites	satellites in **geo-stationary** orbit
global warming	The name given to the fact that the average temperature of the Earth is increasing.
gravitational force	attractive force between two **masses**
gravitational potential energy	energy a **mass** has because of its height
greenhouse effect	a natural process that keeps the Earth warm

greenhouse gases	the gases that cause the **greenhouse effect**	**minerals**	chemical compounds found in rocks
head (of water)	depth of water above a tap	**moment**	perpendicular force multiplied by distance from **pivot**
herbivores	animals that eat only plants		
hydro-carbons	chemical compounds made up of only carbon and hydrogen atoms	**most reactive**	the substance that is more reactive than the others
		neutralisation	a type of reaction between an acid and an alkali
indicator organisms	living things that show how much pollution there is	**non-renewable fuels**	fuels that cannot be replaced
inherit	when features of a living thing are passed on from parent to offspring	**non-selective insecticides**	chemicals that will kill any insect, whether or not it is eating a farmer's crop
inherited variation	those features of a living thing which were passed onto them by their parents	**nutrients**	any food substances needed by the body, including carbohydrate, fat, protein, vitamins, minerals, and water
insecticides	chemicals that are used by farmers to kill insects		
kinetic energy	energy a **mass** has because of its speed	**omnivores**	animals that eat both plants and other animals
least reactive	the substance that is less reactive than the others	**orbiting**	when a **mass** moves around another due to **gravitation**
load	force that needs to be overcome to do a task	**organic material**	any substance that comes from living things
low earth orbit satellites	satellites which are close to the Earth in their orbits	**pesticides**	chemicals that kill pests
		pests	animals that feed on crops grown by farmers
lustre	the shiny surface of a metal		
mains electricity	electrical energy supplied through power lines or from a generator	**photo-synthesis**	the chemical reaction that occurs in plants where water and carbon dioxide react, in the presence of light and chlorophyll, to make glucose and oxygen
mass	amount of matter		

physical weathering	rocks being weathered by changes in temperature	**salt**	an acid that has had its hydrogen replaced by a metal
pipette	a very accurate device for measuring out a fixed volume of liquid	**Sankey diagram**	way of showing the flow of energy
pivot	point around which something turns	**satellites in highly elliptical orbits**	satellites that have an orbit which takes them close to and far away from the Earth in each orbit
polar satellites	satellites that have orbits that take them over the North and South poles	**selective breeding**	choosing a desirable feature in living things, and breeding over several generations so that all offspring have that feature
pollen cell	the male sex cell in plants		
pollutants	substances that harm the environment		
potential mechanical energy	energy stored mechanically as in a spring	**selective insecticides**	**insecticides** that only kill particular types of insect
power rating	a measure of the number of joules per second an appliance uses	**sexual reproduction**	the type of reproduction involving formation of sex cells, **fertilisation** and formation of a zygote
pressure	force divided by area	**speed–time graph**	graph that shows how speed changes with **time**
principle of moments	where all **moments** on a system cancel out	**sperm cell**	the male sex cell in animals
producers	plants that make their own food using energy from the sun	**sprain**	an injury caused by stretching a ligament
		strain	an injury caused by hurting a muscle
reactivity series	a list of substances in order of reactivity, usually most reactive first	**streamlined**	shape that moves through air or water with little resistance
renewable	a fuel that can be replaced	**strength**	of acids: the pH of an acid. Strong acids have low pH numbers
respiration	the chemical reaction which releases energy from glucose. The reaction also uses up oxygen, and produces carbon dioxide and water	**surface area**	the total area across which substances can be absorbed

sustainable	farming that does not involve the destruction of the environment	**transferred**	energy moved from one place to another
symbol equation	a way of using chemical symbols to represent a chemical reaction	**transformed**	energy changed from one form to another
		turning effect	how large the **moment** on a system is
tarnished	said of a metal that has lost its **lustre**	**voltage**	measure of electrical push
theory of conservation of mass	theory stating that atoms cannot be created or destroyed during a chemical reaction	**voltmeter voltage**	a device for measuring
		volts	unit of electrical **voltage**
time	how long something takes	**weathering**	the process of changing rocks due to natural processes
toxins	poisonous chemicals	**weed killers**	chemicals that kill weeds
trace nutrients	**nutrients** that are only needed by plants in very small amounts	**weeds**	a plant that has started to grow where it is not wanted
		weight	force on something due to a **gravitational field**

Index